# TALES FROM THE MARGARET MEAD TAPROOM

# TALES FROM THE MARGARET MEAD TAPROOM

by Nicholas von Hoffman
and Pulitzer Prize winner
## Garry B. Trudeau

**Sheed and Ward, Inc.**
Subsidiary of Universal Press Syndicate
Kansas City

*Tales from the Margaret Mead Taproom.*
Text copyright © 1976 by Nicholas von Hoffman
Illustrations copyright © 1976 by Garry Trudeau

**Library of Congress Cataloging in Publication Data**

Trudeau, G          B          1948-
    Tales from the Margaret Mead taproom.

    1. American Samoa—Anecdotes, facetiae, satire,
etc. I.   Von Hoffman, Nicholas.   II.   Title.
PN6728.D65T78 1976        818'.5'407        75-17055
ISBN 0-8362-0631-2

"I coveted that post for many years. For a while it was my only ambition. I pursued it relentlessly, and at one point in either 1964 or '65 it seemed within my grasp. Larry O'Brien, now the chairman of the Democratic Party, was the man in charge of pork-barrel/patronage appointments at the time, and he gave me excellent reason to believe my application was on the verge of bearing fruit . . .

"As it turned out, O'Brien pulled a fast one on me. He never had any intention of making me Governor of American Samoa, and when I finally realized this it made me very bitter and eventually changed my whole life."

Hunter S. Thompson
"Fear and Loathing:
On the Campaign Trail '72"

To Larry O'Brien

# Contents

# 1/ Seven for Samoa

*Seven for Samoa*

Garrybaldi wanted to go to Samoa because the Nantucket Kiteman had made up a batch of special South Sea kites. There were other reasons.

He'd drawn and written extensively about American Samoa, so now it was time to do some research on the subject. Today's responsible journalism demands that you have your facts right, if not before you go to print, at least afterward. Garrybaldi is a B-52 pilot of the drawing board. He may drop them blind from ten miles up, but he likes to get down on the ground occasionally to check out the damage.

I had my reasons, too, but I don't remember them. I do remember calling Garrybaldi from a motel room in Austin, Texas, at four o'clock in the morning to inquire what was up and being told that he was going to Samoa. I must have said, I'll come too, and presumed one or the other of us would be sensible enough to chicken out. As the younger and more mature person it was up to him to do so, and since he didn't, the responsibility for the prose part of this work is mostly his.

Why did Jim Davidson come? He'd recently been prospecting for a banana mine in Costa Rica and thought he might have better luck in Samoa. As a jogger of some note he hopes someday to be able to say he has literally run all over the earth, and then, as head of the National Taxpayer's Union, it's his job to ferret out and expose government waste, inefficiency, and corruption everywhere. Other ferrets with a knowledge of what hell living on that island paradise is preferred waste, inefficiency, and corruption to going there to investigate it. Outside of a clerk snitching an air conditioner from a government warehouse, there's nothing to steal in

Samoa but money and there's nothing to spend the money on.

Elizabeth Ashley, our leader, the Delta Queen, our star, asked only for (1) an island, (2) white sandy beaches, (3) palm trees, and (4) sun. She got what she asked for only not in even amounts. There were three days of sun, 175 degrees on the beach, then the rains came for six days, and then we left.

Until she hit Samoa, Liz thought she had an affinity for tropical islands, that she and they got along together, but her experience had been all Caribbean where they are used to gringos and they don't have the cockytail lounges like Evalani's, where they're "featuring Keri, A Professional Bartender From Los Angeles."

Christian came because when you're seven years old and your mom goes on vacation you go with your mom. Christian had a good time. He found people to play with even when the adults didn't. He would float around the swimming pool clamped on to Garrybaldi telling him stories about virtuous orphans and unhappy old ladies. Christian did okay and when he misbehaved he was pretty nice about it.

Jim McCarthy didn't misbehave and he was pretty nice about it too. He came to be with Liz and play the guitar and because he's a man for seeing things once anyway.

The Rock 'n' Roll Floozy came for reasons you can read about later. She was the only one of us to undergo a magic experience which made a new woman out of her when she resumed her life back in L.A. Davidson kept running, kept in shape, and kept away from the falling coconuts, so he came back primed with the most scandalous facts and imperviously the same. McCarthy and Liz returned scarred and in love, but life does that.

Only Garrybaldi and I came home limping. I was cured by room service at the Beverly Wilshire. He put himself in the Yale University Hospital in New Haven, where his fellow Old Blues couldn't figure out what was wrong with him though they sent him a huge bill anyhow. They discharged him out onto the streets sick and shaking, but three days without medical attention cured him and now we're thinking we had such a good time that next year maybe it'll be seven for Ouagadougou.

16

# 2/ The View from the Sadie Thompson Cocktail Lounge

*High winds over Mount Alava*

*"The do-gooders regard it as the manifest destiny of America to confer the benefits of the New Deal on every Hottentot."*
Senator Robert A. Taft, 1943

"Nothing works," the army captain said the way all *palagi* do when what they mean is that Samoans can't make anything work. The lights in the Sadie Thompson lounge had just flickered and extinguished in the rest of the Pago Pago Americana and across the whole of the island for all we knew.

"Warm beer tonight," a *palagi* at another table shouted at this reaffirmation of native incompetence. When a *palagi*—pronounced palangi just as Pago Pago is Pango Pango—has been on this green and volcanic isle long enough to take its beauty for granted, there are only three things for him to hold on to: sex, alcohol, and belief in the innate incapacity of the thirty thousand brown people they have been called on to rule over, guide, develop, teach, protect, and generally mess around with.

The captain, however, wasn't a typical *palagi* shipwreck, one of the bureaucratic beachcombers serving out the years of his contract with Gas (Government of American Samoa). He was a visitor waiting for his plane to take off in a few hours, here on a mission "I can't discuss," as though there are any secrets on this island for those whose curiosity is strong enough to overcome the wet and the heat.

The last day of his visit had been frustrating. "I had an urgent need to contact Tonga, but you know it's impossible to communicate with Tonga from here," he said, getting ready to expatiate on the nothing-works theme.

The real question is why an army man would want to communicate with Tonga. Located about five hundred miles south of here, it is the only island group in the Pacific with less military significance than the one the captain was on. Conceivably he wanted to talk to His Majesty, King Taufa'ahua Tupou IV. Polynesians run to impressive sizes in the eyes of *palagis*, who are used to talking about little brown people and are uniformly surprised to see big, little brown people: but Tupou IV, who is reputed to weigh in at eight hundred pounds, is impressive by any standard.

Several years ago a group of well-to-do Libertarians, under the code name Project Minerva, had sought to put all their gold, their freeze-dried food, and their women on yachts and seize one of the islands constituting Tupou IV's dominions but had been foiled either by the outrigger warships of His Majesty's fleet or by an unlooked for wave. So perhaps the captain was trying to call Tonga to negotiate a mutual defense treaty to be activated in the event of another attack by chiliastic right-wing radicals, Seventh Day Adventists, or other American millenarians looking for a safe haven against the day when Jeane Dixon predicts their own society will fall into lawless anarchy.

"I tried to raise Tonga all day," the captain repeated, "and these people here didn't care. The phones were out the entire morning," he announced in tones of such genuine indignation you would have thought he didn't know that the phone company is owned by Gas and nothing Gas owns works.

"One lame, lying excuse after another. The only man who could fix it was visiting a cousin in Hawaii, and then when he showed up he didn't have the right tools, and then it was time for lunch, and then," the captain continued, drinking his gin and tonic and enjoying these renewed proofs of incompetence, "when the service was restored, they told me they had bad news; they said they were having one of their holy hours and no one was on duty."

The holy hour, or Sa bugs most *palagis*. For fifteen minutes

at suppertime everything on the island is supposed to stop for meditation. If you happen to be on the road during Sa, you're expected to flop down under the nearest palm tree to pray or contemplate the eternal verities. At home you are to go indoors or into your Polynesian hut or *fale* and observe the rule of silence.

Around the concrete beehives of pseudo-Polynesian design which constitute the *palagi* compound at the Pago Pago Americana, Sa is not observed. Everybody goes on drinking, but comes 6:30 elsewhere on this little island of fifty-two square miles you had best do as the natives do. George Wray, a *palagi* lawyer, says he was fined five bucks for drinking Scotch on his front porch during Sa, and in our party Liz, McCarthy, and the Rock 'n' Roll Floozy got themselves stoned (by people throwing small rocks) when, innocent of knowledge of the local customs, they drove through a village during the silent hour.

Throwing stones is a traditional Samoan way of expressing displeasure, contempt, or annoyance at children, dogs, strangers, or transgressors of one sort or another. Raise your hand as if you might be ready to throw a stone in front of any dog on the island and it will take off as though you'd tied a firecracker to its tail. In the past, Samoans may have stoned people to death—we only came across one allegation of contemporary stoning of a human being—but they will still sometimes chuck them in your general direction if you misbehave.

Stoning is but one of many customs which earn the criticism of the *palagis*, who come from a culture where the sanctioned form of disapproval is the revolver. No one, of course, would dream of chucking pebbles in the direction of the captain, even if he was gross enough to insist on calling up Tupou IV during Sa. The captain is a welcome figure on the island, for he heads one of the military recruiting teams which regularly visit Samoa to extract from this little colony—the only American possession south of the Equator—its single natural resource: soldiers.

"We recruit the hell out of them," the captain explains, forgetting he is sailing under sealed orders not to discuss his mission. "They make good soldiers, but you have to keep them together. If you put one in a unit alone, he'll go kinda crazy on you."

"I may have a $2,500 bonus for you," says one of the enlistment ads in the *Samoa News*, the island's most widely read paper, "Get Moving. Get Into the US Army. Join the 396 Samoans Who Have Already Joined. See Sgt. Dougherty and His Recruiting Team at the Americana Hotel." And they do go see Sgt. Dougherty. It's estimated that 90 percent of the island's high school seniors leave paradise within a year after graduating either to go on welfare in Hawaii or in the service.

However, this trickle of enlistees represents Samoa's only contribution to American defense or offense. Strategically, it is in the wrong place, although, as Garry says, it would be an invaluable base if we ever decide to invade Australia. Since that is a remote possibility, even for the warlike and restless Americans, the Navy gave up its jurisdiction over the island in 1951. Because of the splendid job the Department of Interior had done working with American Indians, it was awarded this new responsibility. Since then there have been no military installations on the islands although our warships have turned up from time to time to pick up stray astronauts plummeting back from the moon, and not too long ago some kind of deputy secretary of defense paid the place a visit in the course of his honeymoon or an international conference—stories differ on that—but there is general agreement that all he did was rush off the plane, eat, drink, buy souvenirs, and jet off in a vaguely eastern direction.

Poor Sacred Hen!—which is what we were told Samoa means if literally translated in *palagi* talk—you lack anything to excite American rapacity. You have no natural resources unless you want to count the Charlie-the-Star-Kist-Tuna factory. In the French colony of New Caledonia to the southeast there are vast nickel deposits, but Samoa is a volcanic rock of fragile ecology upon which grows a green jungle and under which is no mineral worth tearing up the turf for. Samoa is a bit of absent-minded imperialism from which the mother

26

country derives nothing except a place to practice a mixture of action anthropology and madcap social welfarism.

The five major islands (there are also two atolls and six islets) composing American Samoa do have certain other functions. They afford a small number of young teachers with the illusion of dedication to a backward people; they offer others a chance to lead the life of beachcombers and scuba divers on a government salary while providing a haven for a corporal's guard of losers, romantics, snivelers, closet racists, alcoholics, adventurers, and miscellaneous others who don't realize what happens to Anglo-Saxons set down in the tropics to rule over others of different heritage. Their skins wrinkle and their psyches fall apart. They never learn not to go out in the noonday sun, and they deride what they don't understand while developing a dependent need for derision.

"We'll just rub our two cultures together and hope for the best," Mrs. Ruth, the governor's wife, said. She was serving drinks out on the porch-veranda of Government House. Her husband was off in Washington trying to get some money for the islands new electrical generator. Frank Barnett, the lieutenant governor, was there, as was Don Graff, a young guy in charge of preserving the ecology. The veranda, Government House itself, looked almost exactly like Uncle Duke's, which was disconcerting because Garry had drawn it without ever seeing a picture of Samoa. Those late show movies starring Ronald Colman and Tyrone Power in the colonies were accurate.

Mrs. Ruth is the kind of lady who is able not to hear the nagging drums—old oil cans beaten with sticks—unless it is an official ceremony when you are supposed to hear them and tell the High Talking Chief how nice they sound. A North Carolinian who had to endure her husband's three terms as a congressman in Washington, she is up to handling Samoa and smart enough to know that the best thing she can do in this high-ceilinged mansion, built for naval officers in starched whites, tall collars, and binoculars, is to try and carry on a normal American family life under the slowly revolving fans.

"They're wonderful people; I'm going to love them. We're

dedicated to these poor people, but what they call sharing we call stealing,'' she said, putting down a plate of hot hors d'oeuvres, and recounting how she'd lost her valuable Spanish fan at the inauguration. Samoan dishonesty and petty theft is especially visible to the *palagis*, coming as they do from a virtually crime-free society, but despite the loss of the Spanish fan and the usual daily cloudburst, the inauguration of Earl Ruth as the forty-seventh American governor was a successful occasion, if only because the governor-designate showed up to be sworn in, which seems to have been more than some of his predecessors managed to do.

It was one of those double ceremonies with Ruth, a tall plowboy of a man with feet the size of Ronald McDonald's, taking the oath of office from Associate Justice Leslie Jochimsen, after which High Talking Chief Fofo Sunia took over and installed the ex-basketball coach as the traditional paramount chief of these parts. This ceremony is supposed to include the bringing forward of a *mo'isu'i*, or green coconut, the contents of which are poured over the honored one's head.

A *palagi*, of course, has no way of knowing how traditional these ceremonies are, or whether the fellas sit around thinking up newer and sillier ones for laughs. The whole island seems to have been anthropologized so that many Samoans can tell you his *aiga* (pronounced ainga) is his extended family group and contrast it with our nuclear family. Where anthropology ends and the leg pull begins is something that only the Samoans know.

Frank Barnett, the lieutenant governor, thought it went off well. ''They had a real *taupou* (variously defined as a princess or village virgin), a very high one. Those guys just jumped apart to let her through when she came in there with her feathers on,'' recalled Barnett, a Tennessee lawyer who seems to have gotten his job through the kind offices of his friend and patron, Sen. Howard Baker. ''It was impressive. Two guys were chatting there when they weren't supposed to be and the High Talking Chief smacked 'em.''

Foots, to call the governor by the nickname he's known by back home, had to give a speech. It was an optimistic one,

quite in accordance with the prevailing tone in the nation's Capital eight-thousand miles away. There is a point though when optimism can slip into well-intentioned prevarication and Foots may have reached it when he said, "Don't be misled by the distance from here to Washington. President Ford and Secretary Morton are extremely interested in you and what happens in Samoa. If I were not positive of this, I would not be here."

A man who's had to make his living giving locker room pep talks to basketball players can be forgiven this bit of hyperbole but the truth is nobody in Washington has ever cared much about Samoa. William McKinley annexed Samoa by executive order in 1900 and Congress was so interested in the place it didn't get around to concurring with the takeover until 1929.

Forty-six years later they poured the milk of the green coconut over Foots's head and Mrs. Foots was explaining to Garry and me she didn't like having a lot of servants around. "I only have one housegirl. I shouldn't call her a housegirl," she admonished herself. "She's my friend." Mandatory, contorted egalitarianism. We admired Mrs. Foots for trying, especially since there aren't twenty *palagis* in the world who cared what she called her housegirl or whether or not she taught her how to cook *palagi* hors d'ouevres: "I don't let her do the big things. I really don't like anyone in my kitchen but I let her stir and I'm trying to show her how, but I don't let her put in the ingredients for fluffy things like this."

A modest missionary endeavor. It was easier to understand what she was doing here than what we were. She went where her husband went. The former dean of students and athletic director of Catawba College and mayor pro tem of Salisbury, North Carolina, had been defeated for re-election although both he and Mrs. Ruth walked their feet off giving away Baby Ruth candy bars in the campaign just like they had the three times they'd won. Afterward, when Rogers Morton had appointed him governor of American Samoa, he's supposed to have said, "Where is it?" which is probably what the forty-six previous governors said on getting the news.

They gave him a map before they sent him out here. That didn't cut any ice back in North Carolina, where the *Charlotte Observer* laid it on about his lack of qualifications for "the $45,000-a-year post, with paid-for mansion, limousine and staff that go with it . . . He's never been there, doesn't speak Samoan, and admits that until recently he knew nothing about the South Sea island's culture and government." The mansion's okay, perfectly sited overlooking one of the world's most beautiful harbors, but it isn't really very grand, and the limousine is a non-new Ford LTD; the staff is mostly the housegirl/friend who can't make hors d'oeuvres and anyway, on an island with forty-three miles of paved roads, it's hard to make a big deal of yourself unless you're the King of Tonga or Foots's predecessor, John Haydon, who made an ass out of himself riding in the back of the LTD with motorcycle escort.

Actually Foots is the best qualified governor since Uncle Duke, although he's not the sort to be throwing the *taupous* into the volcano. Moreover, Mrs. Foots is certainly more of a help than Zonker, Uncle Duke's light-headed nephew who came like most *palagis*, not to serve but in search of the perfect suntan. "They're all Christians, but they don't behave in a Christian manner. They'd just as soon throw a rock in your face as not," Mrs. Foots said. Zonker doesn't know the Samoans any better.

Most *palagis* don't. They can't. All the briefings in the world won't help because this deal isn't like an American in Paris where if you know the lingo you basically know what's going on. The Samoans may be Christians—the membership claims of the various Christian churches added up to 105 percent of the population, which is real piety—but this is a different civilization. No gesture, no act, no symbol can be accessible to the auslander or vice versa.

Most often the common bond is gentle, mutual ridicule. *Palagi valea*, crazy whities or sky bursters as we're told *palagi* literally translates into English. That's what they call us and the *palagis* sit around the Americana and laugh about the time the Polynesian waitress served a sundae with an

onion on top of it because they'd run out of maraschino cherries. Did she know better or was that an act of guerrilla warfare?

Mrs. Foots can't tell, we can't tell, and they say Margaret Mead couldn't tell either, that they were putting her on when she was here. Or maybe she got it right but the Samoans are embarrassed as they obviously are about such things as their ancestors using missionaries as a dietary supplement.

Who knows what's going on? One day Garry and I went to the boxing matches. Hundreds of brown people in wrap-around skirts called *lavalavas*, everyone polite and friendly, but we didn't know what they were saying to each other. The boxing match begins with the two fighters bowing to each other and everything looks very American and recognizable down to the brand name on the gloves, Everlast, except the crowd is completely silent. No Samoan equivalent of "Get 'em, Tiger!" Absolute silence. Are these the world's most knowledgeable boxing fans, so taken up with appreciation of technique they won't spoil their concentration by cheering? Then one of the fighters lands a good blow and the entire place breaks out laughing. Funniest damn thing they ever saw. Another blow is struck and there's more laughter. At the end of the round, universal applause. Now what does all that mean? We never found out.

Samoans laugh. They laugh when you say hello and they laugh when they're standing around an automobile accident looking at a bloody body that got itself killed by going through the windshield. Maybe they think things like that are funny or maybe they're nervous. There are so many ha-has, chortles, and giggles on the island you can see where the tittering, sweet Polynesian maidens in the travel brochures came from.

They could also be laughing at us. All this mirth makes the *palagis* uneasy. "They'd just as soon laugh or throw a rock in your face as not," Mrs. Foots told us, expressing the pervasive nervousness of the honkies living among people whose every gesture is unknown and incomprehensible.

If the Samoans were smaller they could be dismissed: "Everything about them is gigantic, even their heads. They'll have a skull the size of a watermelon, with a couple of little squinty eyes and a little mouth and a couple of nose holes stuck in and no neck at all. From the ears down, the big yoyos are just one solid welded hulk, the size of an oil burner . . . They just start out at about three hundred pounds and from there they just get wider.''

They don't, of course, but that's how they looked to Tom Wolfe and to the Americans on the island who expect a spear to come yanging through the mosquito net one night to signal the beginning of the Zulu uprising. Whitey's trouble with the Samoans is that, although he still thinks he's a superior being, he's no longer sure that the natives agree. To *palagi*'s frightened eyes, the best solution is to get these big mothers under contract to the National Football League, where they can be hostile without being political.

It would help if a few more *palagis* spoke Samoan. There's supposed to be one guy in the Public Works Department who drives a truck or something who does, but the only gringo around the governor who can handle the lingo is Rob Shaffer, who grew up mixing in with the Samoan colony in Oceanside, California, and developed a taste for it. Rob came out here as a teenager and then as a Peace Corps volunteer and may be the only articulate, halfway sane *palagi* who knows what the local folks think about us, and he, at any rate, doesn't regard the island as Bed-Sty in the tropics. "The Samoans have never thought we're super studly guys," he says, "but they've always thought we were clever and they know we're powerful. I have a friend in Western Samoa (an independent state comprising most of this archipelago with a population of 150,000 whose only distinction to Western minds may be that Robert Louis Stevenson is buried there). Iasepi told me once about waking up and going down to the beach one morning during World War II and seeing the whole American battle fleet. They were assembling for one of the big invasions like the Marianas. He said he never forgot that day. They know we're strong, but they think it's our machines, which they don't get too excited about any more. When the moonshot came down here off the island, the *palagis* were excited, but

the Samoans weren't that impressed. They see 747's coming in and out of here and they figure if the *palagis* can fly to Hawaii, why shouldn't they fly to the moon? One thing I can do, which I've never seen another *palagi* do, is climb a coconut tree. That really blew their minds. I wrestle with 'em and pin 'em even though they're bigger than me. I know the holds and they don't. They have a lot of respect for that.''

Samoans enjoy wrestling and boxing and every other form of sport. As fast as the *palagis* have introduced a game, the Samoan men and women have taken it up. There are days when the island looks like a vast training camp, a huge Olympic village. It begins at four o'clock in the morning with the boat crews out doing their roadwork. Every Samoan village sponsors a boat, long forty-four-man affairs whose rowers practice with the diligence we associate with North Korean infantry. Then through the day there is baseball, football, tennis, nine holes of golf on the Lavalava course, rugby, soccer, and cricket. The different teams wear different colored skirts and can be seen marching from one athletic contest to the next singing a capella as they go. The Samoans are the Welsh of the South Seas, and although McCarthy and the Flooze were somewhat skeptical of their ability to keep time, their songs delight the ear as their cricket matches do the eye. The Samoan women play cricket with large triangular-shaped bats. When the batswoman—ladies of all ages play—isn't swinging, the members of both teams are clapping out a rhythm in time to the beat of a small boy with a whistle, a tin can, and two drumsticks.

There aren't many *palagis* who can keep up with that, but Rob says that the Mother Country's reputation for athletic accomplishment has grown with the introduction of television: ''They saw football on television and finally got a look at some *palagis* who're as studly as they are and like to hit as much.'' The Samoans can also look at themselves belting each other about the gridiron because Pago Pago TV is set up to do live remotes of the high school football games.

Television is just as popular as sports and the only thing on the island that seems to work. It is also the cause of continuous debate. TV's very expensive to operate for a tiny welfare state on a tropical rain forest of an island with no tax base but a couple of tuna canneries. Gas would love to cut it off and save a little money, but the one weekend they tried they had the famous basketball riot. It was a game between two church teams and Foots and the lieutenant governor had the bejeesus scared out of them. "The whistle at the end of the game was like the signal for the fight to begin and those old boys really went at it," the lieutenant governor recalls.

After that the *Samoa News* wrote, "Some government officials are saying there should be weekend television here at this time when people likely will be more peevish than usual, at a time they will need something to keep their minds off their problems and their arguments off the streets. Although we believe there are bigger uses for such a powerful medium as TV than merely lulling an angry population into lethargy, we can see the government officials' point." Imagine thousands of Polynesians shaking their war clubs, marching out of their huts and climbing onto their *aiga* buses (Toyota pickup trucks converted into mini-public conveyances) and riding into downtown Fagatogo to riot in front of the government liquor store because they've been deprived of "Columbo." Their favorite shows, though, are "Big Time Wrestling" with Moon Dog Mayne and Peter Maivia who has a full tattoo on one and possibly two legs.

Samoa is an all-NBC society, the only place on the globe where Walter Cronkite won't be stopped for his autograph nor Eric Severeid for his wisdom. Conversational allusions to "Kojak," "Mary Tyler Moore," the "Six Million Dollar Man," or anything else broadcast by CBS or ABC won't even elicit a Polynesian giggle. It's all NBC peacockland here thanks to a couple in Van Nuys, California, whose consecration to Samoan uplift moves them to record NBC every night on their home tape machine and ship it by tramp steamer to Pago Pago, where it arrives a couple of weeks later. The *palagis* say that two-week-old television news has taught them to wonder why they used to get so worked up about world events back home; the Samoans do not appear to have a good

grasp on what an event might be. From the time of their arrival about three thousand years ago until the coming of the sky bursters over the round crest of the immortal mushroom cap on which all the seas and islands rest there were no events. Tomorrow is the same as today which is like yesterday so that on this Polynesian island no ready way exists and no need to distinguish fact from legend or John Chancellor from Redd Foxx.

The television transmitter, though, is the most remarked upon work of the human hand in Samoa. The folks here didn't get around to carving any big stone faces like they did over on Easter Island, and the airport with ninety-seven fatalities, caused, it is said, by bad lighting or bad management or bad luck, isn't talked about because it works as well as everything else the *palagis* have dragged in here. To be sure, efforts to make things better are under way. Gas is running a series of executive training seminars for all department heads, and in a way it can be claimed that Samoa has arrived at an equipoise with technology. At least it's the only place I know of where the same number of people lose their lives by murder as they do by traffic accidents.

Samoans are, therefore, either excellent drivers or overly prone to dispatching each other. The fine for drunken driving, the chief of police told us, is twenty dollars payable in thirty days, while that for stealing is five kegs of beer, one fine mat, and two cases of mackerel or so many days' labor on the roads with the village corvee. During our visit we heard of only one prisoner, a rascal who, according to newspaper reports, is incarcerated by day at the Tafuna Correctional Facility in solitary confinement with his television set and his hi-fi but is released at night for the sole purpose of drinking and molesting women. Should he be apprehended reading or studying the moon of the tropics he is liable to more severe punishment under the terms of a Federal Law Enforcement Assistance Administration grant.

The jail being of scant interest there is nothing else to talk about but the TV transmitter. The inspiration for it came from Gov. H. Rex Lee (1961-67) when he saw his little daughter taking typing lessons from a lady in the tube. To turn his dream into reality required the expenditure of an unknown number of millions of dollars and hauling of the transmitter across the Pacific and up to the top of Mount Alava, the volcano whose flooded cup forms the Pago Pago harbor. To bring Mad Dog Mayne in color into the thatched huts of Polynesia, the U.S. Army Corps of Engineers, who are up for building anything anywhere, strung a cable car across the entire bay and on up the mountainside.

They then turned it over to Gas to run and maintain and now refuse to ride on it. Some people do, nevertheless. There are the tourists, who consist of a trickle of impecunious nurses from Aukland and a small number of misinformed gawkers and treasure hunters who think they're in Tahiti and are willing to risk their lives to get to the mountaintop because somebody told them that's where Paul Gauguin buried his ear. A group of Australian vacationers, while hoping to get a free glimpse of Marlon Brando's house, rolled eight hundred feet down the mountain before Hector, the cable car tender, figured out how to get the brakes working. After hours of dangling over the world's most scenic harbor, the Aussies were hand cranked to safety and told Brando lives 2,500 miles from here.

You can't get some Gas employees on the cable car at gun point. But Batman, who runs Gas's two computers, defies the sign on the wheelhouse: "PLEASE DO NOT STOP CAR OVER VESSELS IN HARBOR. THE GOVERNMENT IS NOT INSURED FOR THIS TYPE OF DAMAGE." He goes up, waits till the wind is right, and jumps off in his hang glider.

Garrybaldi insisted we go over on the damn thing. He thought it might be a good place to fly one of the Nantucket kites. Davidson wanted to come because he thought it would yield fresh evidence of government corruption, inefficiency, and waste. Davidson has spent his adult life discovering new instances, great and small, of government corruption, inefficiency, and waste and it never ceases to astound and enrage him. It's either idiocy or optimism, but his emotional life is now dependent on these discoveries. Three months of frugality and probity by the authorities would kill him.

I came along because Garrybaldi made me. I was so sick with fright I couldn't look out of the windows of the swaying car so I sat on the floor and stared at a Samoan woman who was nursing her baby. "That's an adorable papoose you have there, Madame," I said so I wouldn't have to think about what was below. She tittered. "They don't have papooses, candy ass," Garrybaldi admonished me.

Fly your kite, you lunatic.

# 3/ Manifest Destiny in Pago Pago

Davidson goes jogging

"The Hawaiian pear is now fully ripe and this is the golden hour for the United States to pluck it," John L. Stevens, the American minister to Hawaii wrote his boss Benjamin Harrison in 1893. The mob of missionaries, land speculators, sugar monopolists, and thieves represented by the Hon. Mr. Stevens were a trifle too grabby for incoming Pres. Grover Cleveland who made the American adventurers give the islands back. But in 1898, the temptation to pluck the Hawaiian pear overcame any residual national shame and the Pearl of the Pacific was annexed, causing Queen Liliuokalani, Hawaii's last monarch, to cry out, "So it happens that, overawed by the power of the United States to the extent that they can neither themselves throw off the usurpers, nor obtain assistance from other friendly states, the people of the islands have no voice in determining their future, but are virtually relegated to the condition of the aborigines of the American continent."

The Samoans, our other subject Polynesian people, didn't go that route. There was no scene in the White House Oval Room between President William McKinley and Wilmot Fortescue, his assistant, who would later become mayor of Walla Walla, Washington, Pago Pago's sister city. The president didn't say, "Wilmot, Ah grabbed Cuber, Ah snatched Porto Rikko, Ah swallered the Philleypines and now Ah want somoah."

No, if the Samoans are reduced to a status similar to that of South Pacific Navajos, they half did it to themselves. During the second half of the nineteenth century the islands were infested with German, American, and English freebooters, whalers, bible-touting clergymen, traders, and intriguers, all trying to secure commercial and spiritual dominance for themselves and political sovereignty for their countries. The result was a succession of coups, civil wars, and dynastic struggles, mostly instigated by the krauts, so that the inhabitants repeatedly petitioned the United States to take Samoa over. In due course, after numerous courtesy visits by western warships, various landings of marines, snarls, scratches, incidents, and agreements that broke down, a conference was held in Washington at which Imperial Germany got Western Samoa, Queen Victoria got Tonga, some stuff in Zanzibar, plus a few other trinkets, and we got American Samoa, the chief advantage of which is the deep and completely sheltered port of Pago Pago.

America reaped enormous benefits from this deal. We got a place for Somerset Maugham to write, a coaling station for tramp steamers that had wandered off course and out of Joseph Conrad's novels, and a possession of such crashing lack of attraction that vaudeville comedians would have called it the Peoria of the Pacific, had anyone heard of the place. Recent Gallup polls indicate seven out of ten Americans think Samoa is a French colony; a Harris Poll survey taken at the same time reveals that eleven out of ten believe Pago Pago to be a dada word invented by Gertrude Stein to describe her hometown of Oakland, California.

Not even America's enemies have evinced interest in the place. During World War II the Japanese disdained invasion of our little colony, limiting themselves to sending a submarine off the coast of Tutuila. This man-of-war fired three symbolic shots in the general direction of Pago Pago and then sailed away. The first landed on a beach, the second clipped the top of a palm tree, and the third demolished the bedroom of the only Japanese family on the island.

To date, the only American inventive enough to exploit Samoa has been Margaret Mead, whose book is now in its eighth printing. Anthropology is unique among exploitive enterprises inasmuch as it manages to leave intact the very commodity it extracts. Nobody like Claus Spreckels, the

sugar baron who grabbed so much land in Hawaii, showed up to do the same in Samoa. Nobody showed up, with the result that except for a few acres deeded over for the airport, the Lavalava golf course, and the malfunctionings of Gas, virtually all of American Samoa continues under the original Polynesian system of land tenure, which no *palagi* who's spent less than ten years studying it can understand.

Samoa may be a Polynesian Indian reservation but the whites can't be accused of doing their forked tongue act with the natives. The *matais*, or chiefs, still decide who may use the land and how, in accordance with tradition, the kinship structure, ideocracy, eccentricity, and cupidity, the patterns of which are clear if you are a Samoan or have a Ph.D. in anthropology.

Some chiefs are more or less elected, others get their titles by inheritance but all chiefs are not equal. There are the chief chiefs, who are the big cheese chiefs, and next to them come the High and Low Talking chiefs, after which there are gradations and subtleties every bit as complex as the nuances to be found in *Burke's Peerage*. The same thing as in Great Britain where Irish titles are inferior to English ones, except in this case it appears the best titles are located in Western Samoa and that Tutuila, the big island in American Samoa, is especially deficient in them since in the olden times of cannibalism and self-rule it served as some kind of place of exile or penal colony. The island of Manua in American Samoa, we were told, is supposed to be rich in high-class titles. That's where Gas's police chief, Tufele, comes from. He's supposed to have the best title around, besides which he gave Garry a police shoulder patch, invited us to stay at his guest *fale* on Manua, and acted like an all-round gent.

Along with the preservation of the traditional system of land tenure, Gas has permitted the Samoan law to exist side by side with American law. The *pulenu'u*, who you might call the chief of the village council, also acts as a kind of justice of the peace and can punish you for such offenses as "failing to look for the coconut beetle." Punishment may take the form of so many hours' work on the village taro plot or fines ranging from a case of canned mackerel or pea soup to two fine mats.

The *pulenu'us*, some of whom are supposed to act more like Polynesian Mayor Daleys than wise and gentle dispensers of ancient justice, are empowered to go around and inspect every family's *fale* to make sure they are clean. That's easy enough if you live in the classic, oval, wooden-posted hut with the thatched roof. During these last years of prosperity, however, Samoans who could afford it have been inclining toward *palagi*-style houses. Nothing is less dysfunctional than a Cape Cod salt box in a South Sea island palm grove unless it is a Polynesian *fale* on the beach at Buzzard's Bay.

New England homes in Samoa not only require the air conditioning that the *fales* don't need, but they also encourage a *palagi*-like desire for privacy. It's one thing for the *pulenu'u* to walk by the windowless *fale* where the bamboo Venetian blinds are only lowered to keep out the daily typhoon and check out the place with a glance, but to enter the *palagi*-style house unbidden must engender friction.

NBC and the movies are also helping to break down the old ways—*Fa'a Samoa*. They tell the story about the village kids who saw one of those Kung Fu flicks, then got drunk—Samoans have as much trouble handling liquor as Indians and Manhattanites—stole some horses, and pretending to be five Samurai, rode through the village smashing up the joint with the sticks they were using as make-believe swords. Nothing could be more anti-*Fa'a Samoa*. The classic Samoan kid would never act that way because they count for so little, some authorities say, that without the school lunch program they would not get enough to eat in the *aiga*.

Va'asa and McCloud show how when you rub two cultures together you can get pretty babies and lots of friction. Va'asa did well in school and got a government scholarship to a college in South Dakota where she met McCloud. "My father warned me; I warned my husband that it is *different*, really *different* here," Va'asa said, trying to put together by what process of insanity the two decided to get married. "He's a cowboy, he wears cowboy boots and cowboy hats and when he'd walk into the store here the kids would call him Mc-

Cloud. He loved to ride his motorcycle and he'd never seen the ocean, never been out of South Dakota."

McCloud's family, consisting of one mother, one father, and one sister, thought Va'asa was different and the difference was wonderful: "My husband's family would look at me and think, 'Oh, that cute little Polynesian girl with the long hair.'" So they got married, came here, and McCloud found that if the ocean is as limitless as the prairie, you can't ride your bike on it. They were met at the airport by Va'asa's family, just the immediate nuclear one: the seventeen people in her father's household.

With or without previous consent McCloud was turned into a squaw man. When he came to the breakfast table to give wifey-poo her morning peck on the cheek, Va'asa wouldn't let him. "He'd get mad but kissing is disrespectful," she said and might have added that kissing in any form or place isn't *Fa'a Samoa* but strictly *Fa'a palagi*, the word for it in Samoan being *kissi*.

There were other little cross-cultural conflicts that sent McCloud back to the Big Sky Country, such as the custom of a number of unemployed members of *aiga* dropping by for a month or so to be fed and housed. Va'asa's old man would also assess money out of McCloud's paycheck for the native ceremonies. That seems to have been what pushed the marriage on the rocks, but you don't have to be a full-blooded, bike-riding *palagi* from South Dakota to entertain rebellious feelings. It's easier to get a new set of fingerprints than free yourself from all the constraints of the culture you were born in. McCloud resisted openly, and as *palagization* proceeds, youthful Samoan resistance to such practices also grows with it.

The Bureau of Indian Affairs has spent a century trying to make the Sioux take jobs and think in terms of profit maximization like good *palagis*. In Samoa we're succeeding by inadvertence. Six thousand Samoans now bring home a weekly paycheck to the *aiga*. And if four thousand of them happen to work for Gas, that goes to prove it's possible to jump from nonindustrial self-sufficiency to the economy of New York

City in twenty-five years.

With the American Indians we practiced culture-kill along with genocide. The same goes for Samoans' Hawaiian cousins. It's been estimated that by adroit use of venereal disease, measles, Christianity, liquor, exploitation, and neglect, we reduced the Polynesian population of those islands from half a million to one-fifth that number in a couple of generations. As for their culture, what's left besides the ukulele?

From kings to houseboys, but none of that happened in Samoa. The population has multiplied sixfold since Commander B. F. Tilley, the first governor, arrived. He was followed by a string of Uncle Duke-type governors who were satisfied to sit on the porch of Government House in their peacock-backed wicker chairs and watch the locals pop virgins into the volcano.

But then comes 1961 and Kennedy sends H. Rex Lee down to play Big Bwana on the veranda. This boy is a doer, fast with the Readi-Mix and the good intentions. In addition, an international conference of Pacific island nations was scheduled for Pago Pago which looks as it did the day Sadie Thompson checked out of her pension. So let's make with the bulldozers, and he did, pouring a ribbon of highway over a considerable stretch of beach, thereby depriving a number of villagers of parking space for their boats and their toilet facilities.

Your typical Samoan village is situated among the palms, back from the beach, to provide shade and air conditioning for the *fales*. The beach itself is used as the communal crapper. The locals regard *palagi* sun bathing as a form of idiocy practiced by people too stupid to understand what equatorial ultraviolet rays can do to a person. They have other, more practical uses for the strand. Inasmuch as the fecal matter deposited on the white, sandy beaches is biodegradable, the Samoans have themselves a first-rate sewage system. They're still looking for a replacement.

Still, the High Talking Chiefs don't spit on the ground when H. Rex Lee's name is mentioned. There are a lot of people on Tutuila who want roads, among them the owners of the is-

land's three thousand cars—no Samoan statistics are to be relied on—and if most of the stream of Toyotas, Hondas, Subarus, and Sukiakis look like the survivors of a Japanese demolition derby, nevertheless they are driven so energetically on those forty-three miles of paved highway that Gas is putting in for a $900,000 traffic safety grant from the Department of Transportation. Police Chief Tufele says it may even come to a traffic light or at least a blinker one of these days.

One village built its own road not long ago so you can't say this is another case of pouring concrete down unwilling throats. "The Americans have done a lot of good here. The only way you can tell is to compare it to the other islands like Tahiti," Rob, the government functionary, says, but since he's actually gone and lived in the villages of Western Samoa he may know what he's talking about when he says, "It wasn't an easy way of living in the traditional Samoan village. Life is painful. They have a word for it—*tigaina*, very bad. Working in the plantations in the sun, carrying the taro, cutting the wood. It's hard. When I was living in a village in Western Samoa, they had a ship strike in Australia. The village couldn't get kerosene or other supplies. Back to nature time. It was a starve out."

The Rock 'n' Roll Floozy had the first encounter among our party with an aborigine. The Floozy was a last minute recruit. Garry had wanted Candice Bergen and I was supposed to fix her up with an assignment for *Playboy* so she could come along, but I failed to inform either the magazine or Ms. Bergen and Liz was getting depressed thinking about such a long trip in entirely male company.

The night before leaving we'd all gathered at Liz's house in Santa Monica to smoke, drink, snort snuff, eat, and receive the baleful looks of several movie actors who'd been on location in Pago Pago and thought we were out of our gourds. The Flooze was there too and she and Davidson immediately discovered they were companionable health nuts. The Flooze takes great pride in her flat stomach, as much as she does in her voice. Around midnight a meeting of the Board of Directors was convened and it was decided to award her a Samoan fellowship.

The Flooze who is into, as they say, natural foods and natural people, accepted the fellowship on the spot, went home to inform her Laurel Canyon *aiga*, and was on the plane to Honolulu the next evening. It wasn't long after that she encountered her Samoan chief—we never established whether he was a High Talker or what—who showed her his tattoos, a badge of great distinction among the older generation. The Flooze reciprocated by exhibiting hers, a full, smiling moon floating across the clouds on her left hind hip, thereby demonstrating that at least one *palagi* knows how to dress herself properly. "The moon" the chief told her, "has great power," a proposition to which the Flooze would readily assent.

Garry and I met our first aborigines when Rob took us to the village of Sailele. Each of us outfitted ourselves according to our characters, not the needs of the expedition. I took off my suit-coat jacket and my tie, but kept my Brooks Brothers' button-down on and polished my wing tips. Garry dressed more informally, making sure he brought his camera and a very large WIN button (the flasher variety) which read WHIP INFLATION NOW when you changed the angle of reflection. Rob brought along Lawrence Pinter, a *palagi* high school teacher who is writing a natural history of the islands.

Before you reach Sailele you must drive past many villages and a scattering of World War II pillboxes which now serve as depositories for old beer cans. Then the paved road ends and you drive up and over the hills to the other, roadless side of the island where the trail ends, and then you walk. The farther you go, the less the *palagi* influence. Fewer TV antennas and Cape Cods. Cement is never entirely absent, for many of the families who don't live in *palagi*-style houses, do live in what they call hurricane *fales*, that is huts that have cement corners and posts, often with tin roofs. They are the consequence of the 1966 storm which proved that concrete is stronger than wooden posts, plus a government handout of nontraditional building materials.

At length as you walk along the beach you see a small cluster of *fales* that looks so properly authentic they might

66

almost be admitted to the Polynesian Village in Disney World. Tutuila has already mixed its cultures to the extent that anything which is absolutely without *palagi* influence strikes one as artificially preserved with that fidelity of detail you only see on a movie lot or at a World's Fair exhibition. You can't pickle a society any more than you can hold an ecosystem in changeless equilibrium. Things get changed by living. When the Samoans arrived here between two and three thousand years ago, the only fellow mammal on the islands was the flying fox or fruit bat. The Samoans introduced the dogs and the pigs which get Uncle Duke off the veranda to go hunting. The cats, horses, and the cows (forty-four of them by last count, according to Lawrence) are of *palagi* introduction. Who gets credit for *ratus elegans* is uncertain but he stowed away on somebody's boat to do his bit to change things.

We walked by *fales* where there were rolls of pandanus leaves drying in preparation for weaving. The scene with the people inside, and out of the sun, looked like a museum diorama, except that here on the beaches of this South Seas island, the details weren't quite right. There were plastic plates and soup cans, although the flirty children with the loving brown eyes made good the legend of Polynesian entrapment. The kids twinkle for fun and to get their pictures taken. Samoans of all ages emphatically do *not* believe the camera has the power to steal their souls. Garry obliged as one laughing, brown-skinned little coconut charmer asked, "Do you have a Polaroid?" Get back to weaving your mats, honey, Polaroid isn't *Fa'a Samoa*.

The walk was getting to Garry. Ordinarily Garry is a soft-voiced multiple schizophrenic whose various persona are constantly murmuring to each other. The beauty of the spot—the sand, the palm trees inclining toward a blue Pacific, the green volcanoes behind us—and the laughing children were paralyzing him. One by one his characters were dropping away until he changed from his normally burbling poly-schizophrenic self to a completely charmed monophrenic, the first such case I've seen.

In his weakened and tranquilized condition the voices of the children led him off behind one of the *fales* where we found him a few minutes later staring at the world's most beautiful little girl. In his hand he held a large, green orange and pinned on the little girl's *puletasi* was the WIN button. A clear violation of the Trading Trinkets with the Natives Act. He swore he wasn't just another exploiting, manipulative *palagi,* but pleaded the magic of the moment. It was several days later, and only after it had begun to rain around the clock, that Garry got all his personalities back.

With this new insight on the difficulties of preserving other people's cultures, we four *palagis* continued our walk. Rob led us to an oval meeting house in which a man and his chubby wife, who was mostly convulsed by a case of Samoan giggles, bade us sit on the good guest mats and cool ourselves. It's not until you get into a situation like this one that you begin to sympathize with the inspection teams Congress sends out to some far-off place from time to time to find out if they're having honest, democratic elections. They've had three referendums in American Samoa over the question of electing their own governor. Three times the proposition has failed, giving rise to accusations that the appointive governor, Foots's predecessor, had exercised undue, if not almost illegal, influence.

This would have been a good time to inquire. Pardon me, ma'am, we're big-time *paparazzi* from the heartland of the sky bursters, so would you please cut out the giggling for a few minutes. We want to talk a little *palagi* political science. First off, we'd like to ask your husband here if he knows who Thomas Jefferson was. Instead, we talked about the weather, what a fine *fale* we were in, and how we appreciated the hospitality.

As we chatted through Rob's interpreting we learned that the old man outside another *fale* in the rear was the High Talking Chief of these parts. After which there was a certain amount of shuttling back and forth until it was announced that Talauega Lua would join us in a few minutes. In Sailele, as in Washington, the big power man is the last to come on the scene. First the underlings look you over.

While we were being looked over and Talauega Lua made ready, we looked over the guesthouse, which was traditional Samoan in design with American building materials. Some of the artifacts were American too, like the plaque from Fort Ord awarding a son of the family a prize. Lawrence Pinter said the kids in his high school classes always preferred trophies to cash prizes for the winners of the races and other contests. That was more in accordance with *Fa'a Samoa*, but the color decorating the *fale* was American keel paint.

Talauega turned out to be a generous host. He wanted to order up a feast for us, but Rob told him we couldn't stay that long so he gave us each a necklace and pulled up his *lavalava* so that Garry could take pictures of the tattoos on his thighs. Rob showed the High Talker *his* tattoo, an ornate number on his lower stomach that vanished into his pubic hair. Talauega Lua pronounced it altogether admirable as Rob explained that his tattoos, which are very high status stuff, like membership in the Burning Tree Country Club, are done with hollowed-out boar's teeth and ink made from the ashes of a cookout. If Rob really is the last of the New Frontiersmen, he's sure to be the only one with a tattoo *there*. Ethel Kennedy doesn't approve of that kind of thing, but it might help if Garry would tattoo a virgin on Uncle Duke's bald spot.

On the way back from Sailele we stopped at the house of a *palagi* couple who teach at the school the village children attend and got another indication of the penetration of the most diverse American thematic matter in the most unlikely heads. "Last year a student turned in a paper written by Custer," one of the teachers said, adding that he also had a James Bond and a Clint Eastwood in his class.

Samoans have a different view of names than *palagis* do. They take new ones when they feel like it, and considering some of those their parents gave them you can see why they might shop around. Can you picture yourself picking up a small squalling baby and murmuring, "Oh, don't cry little Machine Gun." We also recorded a Televisi, a Remember Pearl Harbor, Rocketi, Apollo, Kennety [sic], Dynamite, Oceanside, Buick, and Chickenshit. That last one could cost a girl friends. "What's your name, Toots? . . . Well, say, you don't have to get sore about it."

Our traveling companions received these nuggets with an increasingly grim sort of mirth. The exception was the Floozy. The Flooze was smitten with the place. One morning over breakfast of hamburgers and French fries at the poolside Fia Fia Coffeeshop, the only facility at the Americana serving anything you'd care to put in your mouth, she confessed that she was thinking about staying on after we left. "A singer can earn a living anywhere," she said, and I told her of an incident I'd heard about in Maine. A hippy girl who'd been passing through stayed and took up with a seventy-two-year-old lobsterman. He'd renamed his boat after her, which bugged his wife, but by most reports it had worked out well. What I wasn't so sure about was the kind of living a singer could earn at the Bamboo Room. It didn't look like they swept the floors very often and the cast of Joseph Conrad characters in there had few of the outward appearances of music lovers. Inebriated old Captain Iaga, with the filthy *lava-lava* and the falling-down-drunk handshake, doubtless meant well but he probably had a tin ear.

Davidson was the most displeased by the island, but he had the strongest constitution. The jogging did that, but it was also the jogging that got him into trouble when, faintly puffing past the Charlie-the-Star-Kist-Tuna plant, a bunch of guys tried to punch him out. It was never determined whether the assailants were Samoans or Koreans who also work there. Some joggers might have been pleased by the addition of danger to this dullest of all forms of recreation, but Davidson was not. Instead he jogged more circumspectly, passing much of the rest of his time reading. He'd brought with him an exquisitely printed, killingly elaborate study of the Egyptian pyramids, which contained the startling information that one of the Pharaohs had been buried with a hard-on. The French scholar who'd written this recondite volume had triangulated this dead mummy's stiff prick with certain other significant objects. We never found out exactly what they were because every time Davidson would show us the diagram we'd all be laughing too

74

hard to pay attention. Jim never understood what we found funny, since as he pointed out, all Pharaohs were buried with hard-ons.

Liz and McCarthy did all right for the first few days when the sun was still paying Samoa an occasional visit. Then the rains came so bad a minister didn't have to meet up with an itinerant whore like Sadie Thompson to lose his religion. The Californians in our crowd, who may have stood on the shores of their semiarid state and wondered where all the water in the Pacific Ocean comes from, learned the answer. The locals said that this much rain was unheard of, but the locals everywhere always say they've never had weather like this.

They told us that despite the fact that Samoa averaged over two hundred inches of rain a year, they'd just come out of a drought that was so bad Washington sent them drought disaster money. We accused them of spending it on flood control. They denied this, explaining that the disaster money was dispensed by setting up a stand by the side of the road where the cash, not checks mind you, but the cash was handed out to the crowd which assembled when the word went out on the coconut grapevine that Gas was giving away something better than free beer. As all the money would end up in the hands of the *matais* under any system of distribution, it was explained that this method saved a lot of paper work. All my life I've heard critics of various government programs say we'd all be better off if the bureaucrats just stood on the street corner and gave away ten dollar bills, but Samoa may be the first place where this advice was acted on.

While Garry and I trotted around acting as we'd been taught journalists are expected to behave if they wish to be taken seriously, Liz, McCarthy, and Christian were more or less marooned in the *palagi* compound of the Pago Pago Americana. After a few days they began to show signs of malnutrition. Their symptoms were those of acute vitamin C deficiency, or at least Liz and McCarthy had them. Christian, being a true cordon bleu, *haute cuisine*, seven-year-old *palagi* kid from McDonald's, thrived on a diet of Coke and hot dogs. Adults don't do as well living extended periods on junk food

but the most scrupulously observed rule at the Americana was
that no fresh fruit was to be served the guests under any cir-
cumstances. Outside the compound was this island dripping
and dropping with pineapples, oranges, grapefruits, mangoes,
and papayas—the stuff grows wild—but in the Rain Maker
dining room, a magnificent chamber decorated with glorious,
hanging Polynesian woven baskets containing plastic vegetation, the greatest care was taken to be sure that not a morsel
was served which didn't come out of a can. The Pan American flight attendants who, like fungi, can survive on anything
or nothing, spent their layover hours in the Sadie Thompson
swilling mai tais, one of those Hawaiian fruit and rum confec-
tions, not for the alcohol but for whatever Vitamin C they
could extract from the Kool-Aid with which the Americana
version is made.

From what we could gather, Samoans who are the least bit
tinged with American values regard the consumption of fresh
fruits and vegetables as the first inch of a backslide into cannibalism. They don't seem to have learned the rule is spinach,
yes; missionaries, no.

Liz and McCarthy had boarded the plane in Los Angeles
with a large hamper of food prepared by the best deli in Beverly Hills, but that was gone by the time we landed, so our
companions were wasting away in the Americana while Garry
and I were out luauing it up in the boonies, getting our Vitamin C and a couple of grand cases of the Royal Hawaiian
Trots. It's not fun to sacrifice your friends' health even in the
cause of our kind of investigative journalism, but we were
having a hard enough time getting any information without Liz
around. Everybody on the island knew we had a genuine
movie star with us, perhaps the first to visit since Dorothy
Lamour. There'd be no way we could elicit information from
these folks if Liz were to accompany us. As it was, wherever
we went, we'd first have to answer a smiling we-know-what-
you're-up-to question like, "You're not traveling alone, no?
Yes?"

Garrybaldi and I had to labor under the unspoken accusa-
tion of hiding a movie star in the Pago Pago Americana. It

only added to the general suspicion that our claim to be bona fide *paparazzi* was a cover story. The only real reporter to hit the island within memory of the living was the poor man who'd fallen so far in disfavor with the *New York Times's* foreign desk that he was made to come out here last year and cover the administrative trial of former Governor John Haydon for referendum tampering. The charges Haydon didn't get tried for are at least as entertaining as those he did.

A Seattle public relations man, Haydon seems to have been another case of life trying to catch up with art. If a man was ever made in the image of Uncle Duke it must have been Governor Haydon. Where, this side of Hunter Thompson or the dwarf people in Garrybaldi's cackling brain, will we find a governor who tried to confiscate a seaplane because it wasn't paying rent for floating on the Pacific Ocean; a governor who used to sit on the veranda of Government House in the ex-Huey P. Newton peacock-chair, a mint julep and a field telephone at his side, looking down at the island's only paved road through binoculars to catch speeders; a governor with an assistant attorney general, paid $36,000 a year, to keep the governor's rowing scull clean by wiping it down with Bon Ami everyday. In one respect, Haydon deviated from the standard of conduct established by Uncle Duke. For, far from being a connoisseur of virgins, in the volcano or out, our man is supposed to have fired one of the members of his staff for fanny patting at a cocktail party.

At the Samoan version of the trial of Warren Hastings, none of these stories were introduced into evidence. The only bar at which their truth or falsity will ever be judged is the one in the Sadie Thompson lounge, where court is convened every weekday afternoon at the Happy Hour (discount drinks) with Gas's *palagi* higher officialdom and their wives perfecting each story for the entertainment of every new, stranded passer-through. Haydon was tried and acquitted at a noncriminal, administrative trial for violating the Hatch Act, a law of suspect constitutionality which forbids civil service employees from messing in electoral politics other than to vote.

He got off on the grounds that, even though he was appointed, he was still a governor and politics is what governors and people like that are all about, so the Hatch Act didn't apply to him. No matter what his job, if he'd tried to pull some of the stuff he did in Samoa back in the Nifty Fifty he wouldn't have been put in jail, he would have been scalped.

At the trial Haydon testified about a Samoan language radio spot urging a no-vote on the referendum to decide if the island should elect its own governor. He described it as a spontaneous, unrehearsed news-program type of statement, but what Uncle Duke didn't know was that somebody had kept the outtakes that had him on the sound tract saying, "Now be sure to get that out and down to the [Gas-owned] radio station and play that at least four times tonight." A similar thing happened to Uncle Haydon—he used to call his wife, Jean, "Mother Samoa"—with a pro-appointive governor television program. Some traitor popped up with a memorandum in the Gov's handwriting that read: "It should be shown to the schools even if it screws up the lesson plan . . . Then it should be shown in the best possible evening time simultaneously on both channels . . . if at all possible. The hell with 'Bonanza!'"

The Sadie Thompson Happy Hour raconteurs have endless amounts of material on the Gonzo governorship: The vignette of the real-life Uncle Duke driving up in the official Ford with the flag on the bumper and the motorcycle escort, getting out of his car and giving his brief case, stuffed with HEW grant applications, to his policeman chauffeur who follows with his hand on his revolver. Another cherished, polished, and embellished story concerns the time Uncle Haydon passed several cans of uncollected garbage on the roadside, which so irritated him he had two of his men take it and dump it on the desk of the chief of the sanitation department, who also was a High Talker so that this act was grievously degrading to his Samoan chieftainship. On the other hand there are a lot of people in New York, Chicago, and other municipalities who dream about dumping their uncollected trash over their garbage chiefs.

For civil libertarians Governor Gonzo wasn't your ideal pick of the political litter. A bit too much of the top kick about him. The Happy Hour gin-and-tonic crowd have mixed feelings about the time Hunter S. Haydon is supposed to have been at home watching TV with Mother Samoa. His disgust at the immorality displayed on his screen grew until displeasure drove him to rise up from the chair, stamp over to the station, kick the door in, and have the technician pull the movie-of-the-week off the air. This test pattern is brought to you by the Hon. Mr. Chief Gonzo in cooperation with the Fa'a Samoa Society dedicated to the preservation of ancient days and older ways.

While darkening the airwaves, he fought and lost his freedom of the press battle with Jake King. Jake King is the owner of the bilingual *Samoa News* and is also by his own description an ex-Marine, an electronic engineer, a lawyer, an Alabaman, a printer, and an inexplicable omission from Joseph Conrad's fiction. In his print shop, cluttered with proofs and parts from the press, his Samoan assistant, his unseen Samoan wife, his collection of Japanese cameras that he says he doesn't know how to use, Jake seems to be there for reasons you'll never know or understand. He has a young *palagi* reporter who came out from the mother country in search of the perfectly honest, crusading, investigating editor whom he says he found in Jake.

For sure Jake and Father Samoa got into a fight which translates into your classic battling newspaper editor versus your bad governor, but what goes on between the *palagis* on this island is a mystery set in the heart of darkness. Governor Gonzo tried to deport Jake. The governors have that right, but so far as we can learn, no successful deportation has ever been carried out. That assistant attorney general told us he wasn't absolutely sure how they would go about doing an official heave-ho. Jake was sued and persuaded by the governor every which way. They even had him up once for siring an illegitimate child. More comedy. The kid's father gets on the witness stand and says to Jake, "I don't know why you're trying to take my child," and Jake says he answered, "Sir,

I'm not trying to take your child; the government is trying to give it to me."

Mark Twain and other cynics in Jake's line of work always have known you can't have a crusading newspaper in a small community, and that's what this is even if the Samoans have multiplied like cells in a petri dish since America got the place. The editor either gets horsewhipped and runs out, or whatever the crusade is gets shrugged off as a feud and a cat-and-dog fight. Gossip is the investigative, fearless reportage of small communities, for talk is elusive and print is too final.

Still, Jake and his newspaper must have played a material part in forcing Ma and Pa Samoa to go home, leaving behind them the Jean P. Haydon Museum of history and older Samoan artifacts, and the memory of the time the Gov tried, according to Don Graff, the ecology director, "to reinstitute the *fia fia* shirts. He wanted everybody in his office to wear those crummy *aloha* shirts every Friday." The Haydons, it appears, weren't insensitive to Polynesian culture.

Was John Haydon a good governor? Was Nelson Rockefeller or Ronald Reagan or is Uncle Duke? What is a good governor? "Haydon used to say, I have only two functions here; one is the money game and the other is to kick ass," recalls our ecology control officer, whose duties seem to consist of finding the nearest places on the island for scuba diving. Rob says he was a hard worker, up dictating memos until four o'clock in the morning. Whether or not anybody read them, Haydon was a lot better at getting money than Uncle Duke. A fast man with a new program, everybody agrees the real-life Uncle Gonzo knew how to tap into the federal grant system. They say he created fifty jobs a month, got everybody off the taro patches and working for the government. Nelson Rockefeller got elected governor of New York four times doing that, so don't knock it if you're on the payroll.

They judge governors and mayors by how well they know the federal rule books, so the question is, should you take your entitlements and get the money off of HEW for nursing-home care for the elderly and the convalescent in a society

where the *aiga* has been performing that task? The *palagis* did it back home and it does make for a more fluid, a more instantly available and flexible labor supply. You can't be transferring people to the Omaha branch if you've got to pay moving expenses for the whole *aiga*. Modern organizations, governmental and private, prefer singletons. It's cheaper and more convenient for the employer, and naturally, if he/she is experimenting with alternate life styles, it means he/she is alone and unable to fight back.

Maybe the best way to train Samoans to take their places in the American infrastructure is to break down the family and destroy the village. That's hard to do with napalm, the use of which gets folks' backs up, but nobody can resist money. Substitute any on-going independent function with a government program and in less than half a generation people won't even remember they once knew how to do the same thing better by themselves. Don't start a Pity the Poor Polynesian Campaign on the basis of that. The *palagis* didn't do anything to them that they first didn't do to themselves.

"Haydon loved the glory of announcing something like a new library and then he lost interest in running it," Graff told us, forgetting the ribbon-cutting proclivities of the politicians back home. "He didn't push operating skills and he built so much and so fast he didn't train people. He had a lack of appreciation of rigor and quality control in the work." But have you ever heard of a band, bunting, and a golden trowel ceremony for a government operation that is quietly doing its job and staying within its budget? American politicians start things, they do not care to run them or know how. The same work habits have been exported to Pago Pago.

Which brings us to the subject of water, electricity, and telephones. Gas is responsible for all these services and is unable to perform any of them. The quality of the service provided by the Gas-owned phone company is nicely revealed by two messages in front of the phone directory. One said, "HANDLE WITH CARE. YOUR TELEPHONE IS A DELICATE INSTRUMENT. WITH PROPER CARE IT WILL PROVIDE MANY YEARS OF VALUABLE SERVICE." The second announces, "If the operator repeats messages in order to accommodate the subscriber because of transmission difficulties, she is deemed to be acting as the agent of the persons involved and no liability shall attach to the Government of American Samoa because of errors made by the operator or misunderstandings that may arise between subscribers because of the errors.''

Now that you know about the phones, we'll tell you about the water. ''One morning I turned on my shower and it came out chicken feathers,'' was the experience of one water user. Governor Foots has solved the problem of water purity. Mrs. Foots boils the water and he carries a bottle of it around even when dining at the Americana. It may not be great advertising but it is realistic.

The Samoan water system works so that the more it rains the less there is to drink. They told us the reason is that the reservoirs are so poorly maintained that the heavy rush from a downpour only serves to clog the exit pipes. With Samoa's annual rainfall in excess of two hundred inches it is possible the islands' population may be drowned while it is in the act of dying of thirst.

It is beyond art to describe Samoan rain. The only reason it stops raining is that if the current storm doesn't get a move on and get out, the next storm can't get in, which would create a meteorological traffic jam back up the Pacific. After three or four days of Samoan rain, you wonder how the natives got brown. Garry explained the brown is waterproofing.

In the familiar fashion of governments, two suggestions are being discussed for providing a sufficiency of water. One is ruinously expensive and the other is ruinous. The expensive one is to eschew modest-sized reservoirs and collectors and seize a volcano and cover its cup with latex to contain the water which otherwise disappears into the porous rock. The bill on that would be up into the millions. The second suggestion is drilling wells, but the saner members of the community like Lawrence Pinter point out that the combination of hydrolics and Samoan geology would soon result in salt water from the sea filling up the wells, so that additional raindrops wouldn't replenish them but would run off into the ocean. So

at the moment they're drilling wells with the usual attendant accusations of graft being made against the well diggers.

Electricity. Sometimes they have it and sometimes they don't. Sometimes they have a lot of it and sometimes just a trickle. The voltage swoons cause more than inconvenience, as the *Underground Monthly,* the only right-wing hippie paper in the world, explained. "Aside from the government's raise in electric rates, have you noticed how much higher your bill is? The reason for this is because of the severe and almost continuous voltage fluctuations we have been enduring. When the voltage drops, it causes the amps to go up. That, in turn, makes your meter spin. Therefore for less you pay more." The voltage drops have a deleterious effect on refrigeration equipment. It's a miracle if there's a single icebox working in all of Tutuila. We did learn, though, that if you kept the light on in the bathroom it discouraged the mildew on the towels. It also encouraged the geckos—a native lizard—that came looking for the bugs attracted by the light. Lawrence Pinter said the geckos have nice personalities, but Garry and I never got on a friendly basis with one, because the lights would go off and the geckos wouldn't come.

Lights? What's to see? Phones? Who's to talk to? You see them all at the Americana, the *Palagi* Palace, that's what the Americana is, all credit cards accepted, use the same one you charge Vigoro on at the hardware store, and, though it doesn't compare with the officer's clubs the British Raj built, it does have a sommelier with a key on his chest and a wine list. Run your finger down the list, order a bottle and specify the vintage. He says, "We're out of it." Try again, he says, "We're out of that." Act exasperated and tell the sommelier, well, just bring me a bottle of anything, Almaden, Cold Duck or Manischewitz. He says, "We're out of wine."

Out of wine, out of water, we'll drink beer for bringing the natives along too fast. It's the spirit of Equal Opportunity Employment. A *palagi* reports that a Samoan in the power department told him, "I never wanted to be promoted, but they kept promoting me and promoting me." Oral history has it that once the lights worked. That was when the power plant

91

was being run by a possibly mythological character named Peasoupu Heinrich who quit when they wouldn't give him a two thousand dollar raise.

It rained so much that one morning at breakfast they ran out of Coke at the Fia Fia coffee shop. That may have been what got to the Flooze. Not that she ever drank the stuff. The Flooze had a way of discovering the one possibly nutritious and tasty dish the Fia Fia had every day, but to run out of Coke brought home how far away we were. Also, she'd been out jogging with Davidson when the rains redoubled themselves making it impossible for her to see through her glasses and he'd kept on running. The Flooze didn't understand Jim believes himself to be invulnerable as long as he stays in motion.

Liz and McCarthy had become young lovers. Holding, touching, stroking, two homo sapiens, sitting on the sand, knees tucked up against their chins, heads on each other's shoulders, grooming each other's hair in love. He had brought his twelve-string Guild guitar with him. We had all fought to make Pan Am let him carry it on the plane. Liz said McCarthy loved it more than her. He would lean down his head and smile Irish, not denying, not affirming. He'd play it a little (he's a picker) and sing a bit, but the Rock 'n' Roll Floozy was stifled in her song, only humming or singing half a verse now and again.

So she said she wanted her virginity back. I offered her innocence, but no, she insisted on getting her virginity back, and said she'd have it if a majority of us would vote for it. Garrybaldi and I were for giving the girl what she wanted. Davidson would snort but would not vote. McCarthy would go with Liz and Liz said she'd only vote the Flooze back a virgin if she stayed one. Thus the matter ended or it didn't. Like making a wish by breaking the turkey's breastbone, it won't come true if you tell.

# 4/ On the Dole in the Tropics

*The Flooze shows the High Talker her tattoo —*

"Half the village may go fishing by torchlight and the curving reef will gleam with wavering lights and echo with shouts of triumph or disappointment, teasing words or cries of outraged modesty. Or a group of youths may dance for the pleasure of some visiting maiden. Many of those who have retired to sleep, drawn by the merry music, will wrap sheets about them and set out to find the dancing. A white-clad, ghostly throng will gather in a circle about the gaily lit house, a circle from which every now and then a few will detach themselves and wander away among the trees. Sometimes sleep will not descend upon the village until long past midnight; then at last there is only the mellow thunder of the reef and the whisper of lovers, as the village rests until dawn." From *Coming of Age in Samoa* by Margaret Mead.

It's passages like that which have given the South Seas their dishy reputation, although you can find a lot of Samoans who'll tell you that Maggy is a crock. There are supposed to be a bunch of old ladies on the island who claim to be the little girls in Mead's book and who say they just made up every kind of sexy story for the funny *palagi* lady because she dug dirt. Since only Mead knows who she talked to and she's never revealed the names, the anti-Maggy campaign could be an effort to spruce up the image. On one level, at least, Samoa is the last refuge and bastion of Calvinism. The boys and the girls may do the hula rock on Saturday night, but on Sunday morning they are all wearing their white *lavalavas* and sitting in the church pews. A part of Samoa is trying to live down its past which is why, for example, it's hard to get a straight story about exactly what happened to some of Jean François de La Pérouse's crew when they made a landfall here in 1787. A bunch of them never got back to the ship and every year the crew of a French destroyer turns up to lay a wreath on the spot where their buddies may have taken the place of the roast pork at the big luau.

That's the thing about Samoa. It is as advertised. You do get the long-haired, brown-skinned, curvy-hipped maidens, but the catch is you may also get eaten. Rob remembers when he was Peace Corpsing in Western Samoa, arriving in the village where he was going to work. It looked like it did in the movies. There were the maidens of paradise, the Sweet Lelanis in the brook, washing clothes WITH NOTHING ON ABOVE THEIR WAISTS!

Appearances to the contrary, Samoa is not a culture that Hugh Hefner got to first. "They're not tit conscious," says Rob, "they're thigh conscious. In Western Samoa breasts are still commonly exposed. The area from the knee to the hip is the real forbidden area."

But that's Western Samoa. The movies, TV, and *Playgirl* have taught American Samoan girls to button up the front. Rob describes the old-fashioned girl as "shy but playfully promiscuous. You grab them in the ass or by the tits and they'll just think it's fun. They don't think you're trying to get them in the sack. With the real jungle bunnies, there's a lot of sex that goes on in the bushes. They cut the banana leaves down, use them as a mat and go to it."

Sounds like fun? There's always a hooker. The female orgasm is unknown in paradise. "I've had girls slip in with me. She'll just lie there, stock still and you won't hear a peep out of her while she lets you do it." Silent sex. It comes along with communal living and fifteen or twenty people sleeping under the same thatched roof. Men and women never show affection. There's no hand holding, no hugging, no smooching of any kind. Husbands and wives don't sleep in the same beds. Silent sex on the sneak. The original wham-bam, thank you ma'am culture.

"I know where missionaries learnt the position," says a *palagi* girl who's given up sleeping with Samoan men. "It was here. There's no screwing in the daylight, but after the third church service on Sundays, at night, they go out, they go at it but with the woman on her back and the man on his knees, missionary position only. They're lousy lovers. You no sooner get your panties off and your eyes closed and he's jumped on and off and is walking down the trail adjusting his *lavalava*. It's over."

The gringos introduced the frisbee, called *i pu lele,* and the female orgasm, the name for which escaped our notes. The frisbee doesn't seem to have caught on but the female orgasm is definitely making progress. Guys sail into the harbor at Pago Pago, find out they have a little something for the girls the local boys don't know about and make a career out of turning grass-skirted maidens on. Actually, the only grass skirt you'll see in Samoa is in the night club show at the Americana for the tourists, such few as blunder in there, and the female orgasm can only be one more disruptive element for a people who've discovered that rubbing two cultures together can cause a lot of heat.

It's easier for the indigenous to forget who they are than to explain it. Like when Father Samoa tried to run the gays out of the bar scene. Who was going to tell *him* that when a Samoan family has too many sons and not enough daughters they solve the problem by switching a couple of the boys and rearing them as girls? Girls do the housekeeping, so converting the boys is the simplest way of solving the servant problem. Father Samoa isn't going to buy that, any more than he will buy the lesbianism in the villages. Here the girls aren't switched over to boys' roles, but from what we could gather in a lot of places there is a village lesbian who introduces the girls to fun and games in the erogenous zone. Lucky thing, too, considering the reputation of the men as lovers, but need we burden the Office of Territorial Affairs, eight thousand miles away in Washington, with that?

The *palagi*-Samoan cohabitation of the island is based in part on a delicate system of interdependent ignorance. The

101

more you know about the other fellow, the more you may get to worrying. It wouldn't help the *palagis* to sleep at night in Centipede Row and Penicillin Row—the names given to the compounds for the gringo government workers—if they were to be told about Laupanini and Paupanana, the Hansel and Gretel types in Samoan folklore.

These two were brothers who ran away from home to live with the wicked witch, a cannibal named Tulivaepupula. Their mother cried, "Laupanini and Paupanana, come back to our warmed-up taro and the big fish we have just caught and fill your little stomachs," but the two micreants replied, "You have whacked our posteriors, so we shall go to Tulivaepupula that he may gobble you up." When they got to the cannibal's house, Tulivaepupula said, "You two shall wrestle. He who is first to be thrown shall be my *kava* snack." Instead of getting to eat one of the brothers, the boys trick him into consuming a lump of hot shit and things work out all right, but for the *palagis* who come already confusing Polynesians with ghetto blacks, it's best they don't dwell on stories like this.

The best method for keeping two peoples in ignorance of each other is to have them cooperate in running a school system. This has worked reasonably well in the mother country with the blacks, the whites, the chicanos, the Chinese, and the rest; but in Samoa, with what we were told was the highest per capita expenditure on schooling in the world, the method has been perfected. To pull it off the teachers must first thoroughly convince themselves of the inability of their students to learn whatever it is they have in mind to teach.

That is best done in a number of ways beginning with the idea that the pupils are essentially frivolous people who prefer form to substance. Hence, a government administrator: "These people get off on ceremonies mostly. They don't do anything inside the schools, but the school patrol boys salute the police cars as they drive by." Next cultivate the conviction that all forms of communication are unwanted and impossible because of the pride and treachery of the natives. Hence, another highly placed *palagi*: "The best thing to do is

to try and not speak Samoan. These people are like the French. They'll laugh at you if you talk their language and don't do it perfectly. You only make a fool of yourself if you try. Their interpreters refuse to translate what you're saying. I went out with a governor to a meeting of chiefs, and do you know what the interpreter said after the governor had finished talking? He said, 'This *palagi* fool treats us like *iti-iti* (children). Don't listen to him. Governors come and governors go.'"Blame it on the culture. Hence, a schoolteacher: "I can't teach effectively because the culture frowns on adults having long conversations with kids. I have to fall back on rote instruction." Another variant of that theme is somewhat more epistomological. Hence, another teacher: "Many subjects can't be taught in Samoan because of the lack of vocabulary. Sciences most of all. Samoans can't handle abstract thought."

The kids' position on this is that the teacher would find their pupils making more progress if the teacher showed up for class. There are universal complaints about late, lazy, and lackadaisical teachers who cut classes, dismiss them early, tell the kids to go outside and throw a ball around, or pass their working hours gossiping in the faculty lounge.

One of the reasons the school system is so successful is that it uses all the advanced theory and technique of a suburban school back in the Nifty Fifty. Disregard such frills as having traffic patrol kids where there are almost no cars, and admire the skillful pedagogy use that television is put to. "Every morning in first grade they turn on the set and listen to math taught in English. The kids don't understand English so the teacher translates what the other teacher on the television is saying, but the teacher in the classroom doesn't understand English either. You don't learn much that way," a Samoan teacher told us, "but it doesn't matter since most of the television sets in the school are broken or locked in the storeroom. That allows us to teach math from books, which makes it easier since all the books are written in English. Anyway, many of the teachers didn't get through high school so they wouldn't know any math even if they could read the book they're teaching out of. The whole thing is a mess."

Reform is on its way, however. The school system is expanding its French language arts program so that soon the Samoan children who can't speak English will be learning French from English-speaking teachers who can't speak French. The physical arrangements within which the Polynesian children are instructed in *belles-lettres* is perfectly designed according to the maxim of form following dysfunction. Faga'itua High School must, therefore, be regarded as a masterpiece of sorts, combining, as it does, the worst features of both aboriginal and *palagi* architecture in a manner that is inversely proportional to sanity. The outer walls are basically *palagi* so that all the sea breezes are cut off from the students. Within, the design retains the Samoan characteristics of openness with none of the walls between classrooms reaching to the ceiling. This facilitates a new kind of multilinear education, that is, a student in any one given classroom can hear what's going on in every other classroom in the building except the one he's in.

A re-hymenized Flooze was up to being told that we'd discovered an entire, complete inner-city school system on a remote tropical island, but Liz was another matter. She'd taken to muttering, "I've paid my dues. I've served my time, I've done my number." It was never absolutely clear what she meant late at night on the balcony outside her room with the rain coming down. McCarthy would be there with a six pack and his guitar, with the Flooze looking off into the gusts of rain distorting the tops of the palm trees, talking like Auntie Vanya, saying things like, "Doesn't it seem like it gets dark here for a long time?"

We'd begun to talk against the Samoans among ourselves. An imaginary Samoan had entered our party and when we weren't quiet on the balcony—ingesting, drinking, imbibing, smoking, and eating—we'd take turns explaining ourselves to him and letting him know what we really thought of his island. "Honey!" Liz would apostrophize him, "I am a Delta Queen who fought her way to Hollywood. I'm not a nature hippie. During the Haight Ashbury I was tap dancing and that must

be understood.''

Garry called us all candy asses. He didn't go native but he stuck up for them even in the darkest hours of rainy night. To buck up my morale he'd insist on our practicing the Harlem Globe Trotters double palm-slap handshake. ''Now, palms go down, palms slap up, no, no, bunny rabbit, I pivot and you slap down. All right, don't be a candy ass, and remember, you pivot after I do.'' That would help for a while, and then Liz or I would start shouting into the storm: ''I AM AN AMER-ICAN.''

We got it into our heads that we'd never get off the island. We'd heard the story about the old tourist lady from Australia who'd been enticed into taking OutRigger Airlines over to the island of Manua with her box lunch. After they landed her, they'd discovered the plane's engine needed its three hundred-hour check-up, so they took-off and left her with her fried chicken for three days. We began to pray to the American eagle. He would land at the airport even if Pan Am was afraid to come down to pick us up and return us home. ''This place makes you believe,'' Liz would say and then howl out into the storm so the eagle would hear and rescue us, ''God, I'm sorry, God, I didn't mean it, God, I will never fuck, I will never take drugs. I AM AN AMERICAN!''

McCarthy is not an American. He is an Irishman and a Canadian, much traveled, a friend of the working man, who, with his guitar had drunk good beer with the best people in the worst places. McCarthy, the quiet friend of the oppressed, would begin his sentences with something about having gone all over the world, the most terrible places, and then, though he never exactly mentioned the English navy, we dreamt of cruisers and armed might. There was a great, obvious, and apparent need of marines, to take us aboard and then destroy the place.

Davidson did not contract a case of white man's burden. As a jogging, nondrinking, nonsmoking, nondoping strong man, he seemed to be saving himself to lead us when the moment would arrive. We suspected him of hiding fresh vegetables and health foods in his room and not sharing, while he looked on our anguish as just compensation for our occasional past support of socialism and the corporate state. Not that he was letting Samoa off. When not running, he spent much of his time in the library reading through the back issues of some sort of Pan Pacific magazine and toting up Polynesian debts.

We alternated between not impinging on each other's privacy, congratulating ourselves on not fighting, snapping at the waitresses in the Rain Maker dining room, and discussing the future of Samoa. Give it to Western Samoa? Would they take it? Make it an independent state? How would it survive? Or let it be? There is another question which had begun to occupy Garry and me. Do any American Samoans live in American Samoa?

According to Rob, a Samoan woman's idea of conception "is that the sperm builds up in her and after a lot of intercourse it turns into a baby. That's why they get confused when they do it just once and get nailed." Notions of this sort can lead to an attenuated and imprecise definition of fatherhood as well as helping to explain why there are so many American Samoans in the world. Add up all the Samoans here on the islands, in Hawaii, and in California and you get a fifteen fold population increase in seventy-five years. This could explain the absence of the female orgasm; nobody would have time to wait around for it. Either the numbers are very, very wrong, or there are a lot of Polynesian wetbacks tiptoeing in the back door.

The wetbacks come from Western Samoa. At the Happy Hour they'll tell you, "This government is run by Western Samoans. Most of the department heads are Western Samoans. Seventy-five percent of the people in it have Western Samoan connections, and what's odd, what's really an anomaly, is that when they're in their own country they run it very well, and when they're in this one they don't. The reason is the bureaucracy. We have three times the money and one-sixth the population."

So apparently the Western Samoans are constantly infiltrating in here spending their cousins' money and gradually absorbing themselves into the American system. There's a lot

of comment about this but not much griping, since everybody, including many American Samoans, will tell you that nothing would get done if the Westerners didn't do it. They are the workers. American Samoa no longer supports itself. Twenty-five years ago it grew all the food it needed. Now it imports, and will continue to until the loaves on the breadfruit trees are baked by Continental-ITT.

This process of migration—first to American Samoa and then to America—is slightly irregular. The Western Samoans are foreign nationals but the *palagis* aren't about to get off their barstools and find out who was born where and send them back there. It's too hot, and this artificially multiplying Samoan population back home represents the best long-term political solution. Since Congress is never going to make American Samoa a state, and Western Samoa doesn't want to absorb seven islands crammed full of demi-Americanized, spoiled, demanding, degenerate cousins, then another accommodation must be found. This one is simple. The population in Hawaii and/or California will continue to grow until they elect a congressman who will represent everybody, including Western Samoa, which will be a *de facto* member of the United Nations.

It will be years before the conservatives get on to what's happening and when they realize there are two Samoas it will be too late. There'll be three Samoans in the National Football League and a Miss Second Runner-Up at Atlantic City. Anyway, the paltry few million it takes to run this mini-welfare state is even lost to computer retrieval from the federal budget. It seems like a lot of dough to the locals, but actually so little comes in here that the money is ragged and dirty. It's not even worth the Federal Reserve Board's bother to freshen up the currency. There isn't a crisp bill on the whole island of Tutuila. People have been living off the same greasy fives and tens that got shipped in here under Kennedy.

The main job of the governor is to keep an adequate supply of moldering money on the islands and make sure it gets spread around more or less in accordance with the local conception of equity. If he does his job well, people don't complain excessively about the few hundred *palagi* employees getting paid one-third more than the aborigines for not doing the same work that the Samoans are able to not do equally well. Governor Foots, however, has a more elevated idea of his responsibilities. Not that he has any grand pretensions, for he need only glance down at the long question-mark shape of his body and look at his feet in order to know that the grandiose would not suit him. Yet he can't hide a certain zeal to leave Samoa a happier, freer, wealthier, and better place than he found it. "They always ask me what qualifications do you have for this job, and I tell 'em the best training you can have for governor is being dean of students of a college," Foots says, unmindful of the political axiom that the best and only training for a job is getting it.

The former dean of students of Catawba College also has a doctorate. Jake King sent away and found out his dissertation title was "A Study of Selected Athletic Conferences in the United States." It tells about the pay scales for officiating at football and basketball games, and there's no doubt that Foots's erudition is helping him appreciate the local view of his job responsibilities. "These folks here have a different idea of money. Squirrels put up nuts for the winter, but there're no squirrels here, no winter—lots of nuts, though—but if the squirrels came here they wouldn't put their nuts up," Foots told us the night we had him and the Missus over to the Americana for dinner. "You leave a country where everybody is hustlin', you come here and you're out of focus."

Foots had gotten hold of the very secret of the thing. The *palagis* come down here after having spent the last hundred thousand years preparing for winter. The *palagi* personality is built around the idea of uncertainty and change. That makes him a planner, a worrier, and an idiot because he's always grabbing some Polynesian and asking, "What are you going to do when it snows?" It gets through to some *palagis* that it is never going to snow and they go completely to pieces. They're the ones who are held together by anxiety about the future. That was Uncle Duke's trouble. Every time he'd get relaxed on the veranda of Government House and start

looking at all that green and blue and realize it wasn't going to change and that there wasn't anything he could do about it or needed to do, he'd go manic-dynamic. Not Foots. The most ambitious thing he'd say is, "If they don't get some electricity and water around here, they'll have to go back to their own culture," which would be too bad, but whichever way it happened, he was going back to North Carolina.

The night of the dinner with Governor and Mrs. Foots was the high point. We were seated immediately in the Rain Maker dining room, which was a big improvement. The service had deteriorated to the point that when Davidson had gone in there for lunch that day they'd told him he hadn't made a reservation and they couldn't accommodate him. "But there's only one person eating in here. All the other tables are empty." So they seated him at the table with the solitary diner, handed him a menu, and told him, "we're out of it."

With Foots, the ultimate chief, there was no waiting, and when he said, "Cool down the air conditioner, Mamasan," they did it. Liz and McCarthy were at another table and Liz was unrecognizable. She'd converted herself back into a movie star. It must have taken her two hours to make up, but somewhere in the boxes and jars of her cosmetic case she'd found the means to scare off the cross-cultural ghosts and return to being an international beauty. McCarthy was slicked up too. It may have been that evening that gave Liz the idea McCarthy should have a suit. McCarthy had never owned a suit in thirty-five years of life. Except for me, I don't know that McCarthy had ever known anyone who owned a suit, and I bag and bulge in the ass and can't keep a crease in the trousers. The suit was for the Tony Award presentations; it was white, it cost six hundred dollars, and was made by the tailors in one of those stores in Beverly Hills where they can tell whether or not to wait on you when you walk in the door. McCarthy never said if he liked the suit. He didn't wear it so much as he went through with it.

This was the night when we let our tribe meet Foots's *aiga*. It was to be after dinner in the Sadie Thompson and the

Footses were looking forward to it. Foots had told us how even if the chiefs were dictators they represented a happy union of authority and responsibility; and he'd asked if we thought he should leave the flag on the fender of the official Ford limousine, so now it was time to meet the movie star.

"Tell us what's going on in Hollywood," Foots wanted to know, accepting a second drink in the manner of one breaking training. Liz was up to it, but she wasn't acting like a movie star. She was leaning forward in her chair, a leg crossed over a knee, swinging a violent nervous foot back and forth, projecting a personality that was anything but cinematic queenliness.

"I'll tell you how I got from Baton Rouge, Louisiana, to Hollywood, if you'll tell me how you got from Charlotte, North Carolina, to Pago Pago," Liz answered in her thickest bayou accent.

"He explained it all in 'Doonesbury,'" Foots replied.

"Had you always wanted to go to Pago Pago?" Liz pressed while Mrs. Foots put her hand to her mouth and laughed, and Ole Foots felt obliged to say, "It's a real challenge and opportunity to serve."

"I felt like that once but they put me in jail a few times," Liz responded, leg swinging, bending her shoulders forward, giving him a long-necked, upward look, "so I just decided I'd put on my eyelashes and do my dance. I always wanted to be an ac-TRESS."

Liz was abandoning us. She was going to get herself and her child off this island any way she could. She was abjuring us. She was turning herself back into a honeysuckle gal, a Southern lady, throwing herself on to Foots for protection. I heard her say, "You know what my mother told me about Yankee men? They talk with mush in their mouths," but it sounded like Liz had all the hominy.

I couldn't tell if she was scoring with Foots. There's more plowboy than Southern gentleman in him, but it was working with Mrs. Foots. Liz had pulled something out of herself that Mrs. Foots recognized and the two of them had begun to feel each other out genealogically. Certain people can't figure out

who you are until they can place you in what the anthropologists call the kinship system. Samoans are like that and so are particular types of Southern ladies. To them the world is a seamless whole, a large but largely comprehensible, lacy network of ultimately interconnecting *aigas*. Somewhere in that conversation both Liz and Mrs. Foots knew they were related, that the one's cousin's cousin's *aiga* would finally interface with the other's cousin's cousin's *aiga*, but it would take some time, being as how Liz would have to start from Baton Rouge and Mrs. Foots from someplace in the Sea Islands and the two of them would have to crawl across the South to meet each other, perhaps in Alabama, but not until they'd established the kithship and kinship of the Savannah Sartoriuses, the Mobile LaMars, the Navells of Natchez, and their respectable Midwestern collateral branches. It's only agrarian societies that have the patience. When the English gave up farming they adopted a simplified method. They just watch you carefully and if you don't handle yourself right, they twitch up their noses into a pinch and whisper, "MIF," and that's the end of you. "Milk In First" is a sure giveaway. When a Yankee lady wants to toss you the snoots, she tells her friend, "NOC," although "Not Our Class" sounds rather *nouveau* unless you keep your chin at the right angle when you say it.

At the bar, a Samoan in a *lavalava* and a white, American-style shirt came to military attention, saluted, identified himself as a captain of police and said, "Governor, I approach you." Liz and Mrs. Foots continued to make their ways eastward and westward across the South. The lieutenant governor volunteered to handle the matter while Davidson tried to establish a conservative linkage between himself and Foots. "I've been making a slight study of Polynesian Imperialism," Davidson said. "Governor I approach you," the captain of police repeated. "In the nineteenth century the king of Hawaii sent a drunken soldier of fortune to Samoa," Davidson continued while the captain of police again saluted and declared, "I approach you," to which Foots replied, "You can approach your governor any time you want."

"Governor," said the captain of police whom alcohol had rendered as stationary as the bar against which he was propping his back, "I am sorry I approach you." That was all right with Foots, who was now taking up his cigar to approach the captain of police because Davidson was continuing his narrative: "But before the drunken soldier of fortune could set sail they had to find a tuna boat or something." I looked at the Flooze who'd put on a slinky dress—I think she'd borrowed it from Liz—so that she was all hips and tits and flat tummy, and it occurred to me to tell Foots or Frank Barnett, the lieutenant governor, they shouldn't feel too badly about the water supply. The Flooze had drunk the magic Samoan waters and grown her hymen back, which is more than I could say it did for me, but then I looked at Garry. Garrybaldi was playing Michael J. Doonesbury, taking everybody seriously, asking viciously sympathetic questions and making nasty little sounds of understanding calculated to lead them all on.

Foots returned from the bar explaining that's the kind of situation an old basketball coach is equipped by training and experience to handle. Whatever he'd said, it petrified the captain into a perpetual salute to his governor, chief, and leader. "They arrived in Pago Pago harbor," Davidson elaborated, "and traded pigs for guns."

"Who did?" Foots wanted to know.

"Then I went to New York and got a social conscience," Liz was saying, as Davidson related, "that a German warship fired a shot over the bow of the Hawaiian tub and saved Samoa. I've found other examples of imperialism by so-called colonial nations."

Foots, who might have been a couple over the limit he sets for himself, looked at Davidson as though he'd just seen him. He had his white suit and his pussy cat bow tie on and Frank Barnett was informing Foots that Davidson, too, was a journalist, down here to do a story for *Penthouse* magazine. Foots gave Davidson another look. "He's writing under a pseudonym, but he's gonna use our real names and he wants an appointment to interview you, Governor." That got Davidson

a third look from Foots, which our jogger must have taken as a sign to continue the narrative of his historical researchings.

"The mistake was made by the first missionaries. They stopped polygamy." Under his breath Barnett allowed as how someone from *Penthouse* might know that. "But before, before," I could hear Liz telling, "I was page for Leander Perez in the Louisiana legislature." Exculpatory credentials.

"They had two types of women: wives and maidens," Davidson said. "But by the end of the nineteenth century, the maidens were eliminated by the missionaries and the cash economy. These maidens were currency when they wanted to exchange land. They were not wives. They were sort of mistresses or concubines, but when they came they brought land. Basically, it was during that period that they began to shift and to give up the use of maidens as a medium of exchange and a store of value, and they began to use Western means of attaining status. By the way, did you know the Eskimos have one hundred words for snow and the Samoans have one hundred for mildew?"

Foots heard it out and then he said to Liz, "Tell us about that crowd that makes movies." Liz was sharpening the pencils of Leander Perez in the State Senate and arranging to come calling on Mizzz Foots for tea and when Davidson began to discuss the eight hundred pound King of Tonga, the Flooze held his hand and Foots rose to leave, remarking that Samoa "isn't like our country. Here I'm away two weeks in Washington trying to get some electrical generators and you come back and your wife takes you to church."

That broke the party up leaving Frank Barnett and me alone. I tried to get the lieutenant governor to arrange an interview for Davidson with Foots. He's your kind of people, Frank, very conservative, right wing. Head of the National Taxpayers' Union, Old Buddy, against all taxes, but the trouble is nobody trusts an organization that espouses a cause everybody believes in. Frank didn't say, "Well they don't pay taxes in Cuba, do they?" but I could tell he was thinking it. If he'd asked how we seven had come to Pago Pago together, I would have told him the trip is second prize in the New Jersey State Lottery.

# 5/ Coming Apart in Samoa

All oppressed colonial peoples have a Liberation Front. Samoa does too. The better revolutionary movements have their romantic aspect personified by someone like Che. Samoa does also. Her name is Sherry O'Sullivan, a young Canadian woman of statuesque proportions, of excited breathy diction, strawberry blonde hair, and one blind eye with an enlarged, darkened pupil which did not move when the other one did. In the tradition of guerrilla fighters, Sherry had spent her time in the mountains living among the people in a village where, she said, "they cut the ears off the women for adultery and they're jealous all the time, fighting over money, titles and sex . . . I saw them stone one man. They broke his skull and his breastbone and destroyed his *fale*." Garrybaldi and I hadn't seen any earless ladies, although that would certainly explain the preference for long hair, but Sherry was the one who'd been living in the mountains with the people. Previous to coming here she'd lived in New York, "doing the painting thing and then I went to L.A. and married an actor which lasted until I went emotionally broke so I took off for Europe and when I got back to L.A. I smelled the air and decided to go to the South Seas the way everybody says they're going to do." For her trouble she's come down with a case of what she calls "green, creeping, mental crotch rot" and is in the process of being deported for being "culturally disadvantageous to the island" and also operating a business without a license.

The deportation proceedings are moving ahead at a speed

129

too slow to measure. "I think they lost my file," Sherry says, but what's really happening is that there is no way to conduct a trial in Samoa according to the ordinary standards of American jurisprudence. The place is too small and too incestuous and the laws are too unconstitutional. Not only is acting in a culturally disadvantageous manner seldom a crime or even a civil tort back on the mainland, but the business Sherry is operating is a newspaper so that trying to license it is a legal impossibility under the First Amendment.

The lawyers and the judges (all three of them) on the island know that, so the strategy is to go through the motions but never push anybody so far that they'll spend the money on an appeal to the mainland. If a federal judge ever found out what was going on in Samoa he'd throw the entire Samoan law code into the fireplace. Samoa, though, can't operate under American law. Polynesian ideas and practices in regard to property, morals, and conduct cannot be meshed with American law and procedure.

The assistant attorney general of American Samoa says, "Our commissioner of public safety probably violates the civil rights, under the American Constitution, that is, of 250 people a day." The commissioner, a great brown coconut in an expensively tailored *lavalava* with an American suit-coat jacket, is our candidate for the first Trujillo of the South Seas, if Samoa should ever suffer the impoverishment of liberation. The 250 daily violated ones make no complaint, because, however harshly he may deal with his compatriots under the American Bill of Rights, in his capacity as a Samoan born, hereditary Big Chief and Cheese, he is acting in accordance with the local understandings of right and wrong.

Sherry rendered herself culturally disadvantageous by saying things in her underground newspaper like, "We have found that Chief Tufele not only has a police record in San Diego consisting of everything from assault, burglary to hit-and-run, but also has an FBI number." She followed that up by printing that half the members of the *fono* (the Samoan version of a legislature) had been convicted of any number of naughtinesses back in the States. Even if everything she

writes is true, a lot of Samoans don't seriously consider any crimes except spitting on the sacred salamander or plucking the tail feathers off the virgin before throwing her into the volcano. Crimes like homocide by automobile seemed to be regarded as civil torts as they were in most European societies for a very long time. One of the lawyers here tells the story of the drunken tourist who ran over a man and killed him. He arranged to pay compensation for the accident to the man's *aiga*, but everybody's mutual satisfaction turned to astonishment when the crazy *palagis* insisted on trying the driver for manslaughter. The state might require the man to go to jail, but the state is an abstraction the Samoans are just getting around to believing in and in the meantime, the *iaga* gets nothing for the loss of a productive member.

Thus, if the rubbish Sherry prints is true, she forces everyone to recognize that *palagi* laws are being violated. That's uncomfortable since they can't practically be enforced anyway. Are they going to throw half of the people in Gas out of office? Try them? Where are they going to find what the gringos would call an unprejudiced jury in a community this small whose members are all interrelated by blood, status, and most intricate traditions? If Sherry is right, the only sensible thing to do is deport her, or at least harass her.

This, she says, they do all the time. One night she was drinking in one of the island's many places of recreation when she says the cops came in and told her that her car was in a no-parking zone and she'd have to move it. When she went outside and slipped the key in the ignition, they busted her for drunken driving. Then she says, they put the cuffs on her, carted her off to Pago Pago's picturesque place of incarceration and worked her over.

In Samoa the revolution orchestrates itself as if Peter Sellers were conducting it, so the guerrillas and the establishment both do some of their drinking at the Sadie Thompson. This permitted Garry and me to arrange a small confrontation between Sherry and the Great Brown Coconut to discuss the matter of the arrest. "We're mortal enemies," Sherry told the top cop as she sat down at our table and ordered a drink. "I shouldn't be talking to you."

"No, no, Sherry, you're my good friend. You learned your lesson not to drink and drive."

"It was a frame-up."

"Sherry," the assistant attorney general said, winking, "you'd have to study six months to pass the urine test."

Sherry also gets it from people like Jake King and the *Samoa News* where she worked for a while. Under the heading of "A NEW LOW IN JOURNALISM" she republished an article that appeared in Jake's paper about her. You don't get this kind of flat-footed, uppercutting, wild-swinging, early nineteenth century vituperation in the States anymore: "The people at the *Samoa News* were really kind and good to her and gave her money to buy soap to wash herself because the people who worked with her couldn't stand her smell. We also gave her money with which she started her paper and she has turned against those who were kind to her and her guardians at the beginning. She is like a wandering woman who sits in a different bar collecting only half her information and truth for her paper. . . . Everything written by Sherry O'Sullivan is a lie because she is good at writing untrue stories and lies. She is well known for gathering her stories in bars and being a loudmouth." A lost art form but by the time Garrybaldi and I left the island we also were well known for gathering stories in bars and being loudmouths. A journalist would have to be crazy to trot around in that wet and heat and risk getting attacked by an overly excited tropical plant, when you can get the same stuff at the Happy Hour while consuming enough gin to protect your health. While we were there an epidemic of dengue fever was reported rolling in from Tonga and, although that is not the disease which swells your balls up to the size of beer barrels, what ever it is, they told us it was pretty gross.

With small nation, insular living, nothing can be pushed to the limit. There is no place to hide and no place to go, so unless you're going to kill your enemies, the best policy is to win but a moderate amount and then take an accommodating attitude. That is perhaps why the Great Brown Coconut said,

"Since Sherry is going to be a permanent resident, I'm thinking of adopting her as a partner. Someday she might instigate a resort."

"Don't you know," the assistant attorney general said, "someday she's going to try to get a Don the Beachcombers in Manua?"

The suggestion that Sherry might be party to sticking a restaurant with a two-hundred-foot high neon-lit palm tree on American Samoa's most "unspoiled" and traditional island was a jab at her and the other members of SLUF (Samoan Liberation Front). The SLUF infrastructure is built around and radiates out of the Pago Pago Rotarians, and as such it is the only free enterprise, revolutionary movement in the world, just as Sherry's newspaper is the only underground publication that regularly receives bank advertising. While the underground press in the rest of the world undeviatingly supports the principles, if not the actualities of trade unionism, the illegal press in Pago Pago has committed itself to keeping unionism out of the tuna plants: "Samoa is an unlikely candidate for such things as unions. Unions work in ghetto areas and in seriously depressed areas. . . . Unions demand that all members attend their meetings. These are held at night [would therefore interfere with drinking]. If you don't attend you are fined. . . . Regardless of whether you work or not, you still have to pay the $9 to $12 per month dues to the union. If you don't you will be fined."

With socialized everything, no land for sale, and almost the entire population on the Gas payroll delivering inessential services inadequately to people who spend their time listening to the fish fart, the Rotarians and allied subversives figure unions'll knock off any chance of developing an economy that might pay its own way. The rest of us in the various far-flung American dominions may look at the Waikiki kitsch condominiums of Hawaii as an ecological felony, but not SLUF. SLUF stands for "sluff-off-tropical-torpor and get swingin'," if we're gonna have a cash economy, then let's make some cash. From Maine to California, embattled conservationists struggle to keep oil refineries out; SLUF dreams of getting one in, and if that won't work, what about legalizing gambling and teaching the girls how to feign a *palagi*-style orgasm for the conventioneers?

It was an impulse like that which resulted in the Americana. Gas financed part of it and a lot of locals also put money into it, but it was a bust from the beginning so with irrefutable logic it was decided to enlarge it. The constant rumor is that American Airlines—the franchise holder which provisions the place with the scraps and leavings of economy class dinners— is going to pull out. They can't be making money. Aside from the Happy Hour crowd in the Sadie Thompson, the hotel looks as if the only customers it gets in are an occasional group of retired Swedish factory workers who only stay long enough to contract skin cancer from sun and grow purple fungus between their toes.

The nightclub act in the Rain Maker pulls them in to see the big guy from Tonga eat fire and watch Rosey. Rosey must come in at around 350 pounds, and with a white flower in his ear, a loincloth, his brown girth smeared with coconut oil, he's something different in Polynesia, dancing on his toes and wiggling his fingers, or, after the show, coming into the bar while he gives his hair a primp and sets his Gucci handbag down preparatory to ordering a drink.

The emcee is Herb Scanlan's mother. They seem to have a lock on the island's professional entertaining. Herb's great-great-great-grandfather was a Boston Irishman who jumped a whaling ship, perhaps to introduce the female orgasm but certainly to found a dynasty, for the Scanlan *aiga* has proliferated in size and accomplishment to the extent you can't walk into a bar without finding Sia Scanlan, or Rosey, or the fire eater or a row of Scanlan nieces in grass skirts doing with the fingers and stamping out hula rock in their bare feet. The Scanlans own a motel, a nightclub, a car rental service, and stores, and Herb's got a B.A. in economics from Pomona. "I'm Talking Chief, I sat in the constitutional convention because of my grandmother's title but around here we really get more chiefs than Indians.'

Samoa may be the only American possession where some

political offices are still hereditary. Garry and I could never quite get anybody to explain it so we could understand it, but it looks like the upper house of the *fono* or legislature has a certain number of seats reserved for hereditary chiefs. But Herb isn't interested in being a member of the House of Lords: "It's a helluva system. The chiefs control the land so we can't have any industrial development. I'd like to see a casino but these guys in the *fono* say what for. Uncle Sam'll take care of us. But he's not going to when the shit hits the fan. Once the land laws are gone the chiefs won't have any way to control the people, and for me and my friends it won't be too soon."

Herb, though, is pretty Americanized and uppity. If you ask him to explain the extended family system—everybody on the island can talk in anthropology—he'll say, "Hell, man, all I know is if they're a second cousin you can fuck 'em."

Even Chief Fui, the ex-delegate and a pretty conservative cat, would like to see a few changes: "There's so much green on this island. I'd like to have a flower-planting project so we'd get some variety of colors." Not that Fui is frivolous. He took us up to his territory, the village of Aoloau, in his Ford LTD station wagon—it's gotta be the biggest passenger car on the island—where we met all the local sub chiefs, serious guys with gray hair, eyeglasses and tattoos on their legs.

They told us that Aoloau was the only village left that grows all the food it needs to sustain itself and enough more to make a tidy income. Taro—a nice, big, fat, happy gray one —will sell for three or four dollars apiece down at the 24-hour-a-day Samoan-style supermarket where the salesladies sleep next to their wares until you walk in; then they sit up, point to their merchandise with a stick—the cowrie shell necklaces, the mats—and say, one dollar, two dollar, or, very rarely, ten dollar.

Taro is one of your acquired tastes. It has the consistency, feel, and taste of congealed milk of magnesia, but Samoans love it, only not enough to grow it. All over the inhabited part of the island you can see abandoned taro plantations. What they call a plantation we'd call a field on a mountainside and climbing up to cultivate them must be a chore, a chore fewer and fewer of the young men can be made to do when they can enlist in the army or work for the government. "Samoans eat hamburgers and French fries," says Herb, who probably dreams of getting the franchise to erect a Golden Arch, the size of the St. Louis memorial, across Pago Pago bay. But he's right. You see Wonder Bread and packages of Hostess Cupcakes in the little village stores while outside along the road the grapefruits hang from the trees unplucked and unstolen.

Once upon a time, the Samoans were a breathtaking seafaring people. They built superb ships and they could navigate across the Pacific, and after days on the water, hit the right fly speck atoll right on the money. Now any fishing that takes the sailors out more than a couple of days is done by the Koreans or the Chinese. Garrybaldi decided not to investigate them after we heard the Chinese were having themselves an old-fashioned tong war over on their side of the Pago Pago Bay. These Chinamen kept turning up head down in the drink, pulled out and certified as suicides by the Chinese doctors until the authorities insisted a *palagi* medic assist at the autopsies, whereupon mental health in the Chinese community suddenly improved. That's the story anyway. They'll also tell you that Samoa has the highest suicide rate in the world. Does that mean this island is more socialist than Sweden, or are people who live in the very hot and the very cold just disposed to doing themselves in?

They're forgetting how to farm, they don't know how to build their splendid transoceanic ships, only the older people, and not many of them, are still able to do the more difficult kinds of weaving, and they're losing the more formal and elaborate parts of their language relating to the old, high culture. "I look on putting bread on the table as more important than putting on feathers and beautiful Samoan costumes and jumping and shouting," says Herb, who is not too terribly interested in ethnographic preservation. He's got a point. After a while you'd begin to feel like a jackass if you went to too many movies like *The Towering Inferno* and then came home,

put on your grass skirt, and started hopping around when there aren't even any tourists to watch. Maybe if there were more *palagis* on the island or they were more openly hostile to Samoan culture, an ethnic reaction would set in and people would go to Polynesian heritage classes. Instead it's just slipping away.

It remains somewhat of a mystery how Chief Fui keeps 'em down on the taro patch plantin' yams and eatin' hams when the old ways and social discipline are evaporating over the rest of Samoa. He says he does it by delegating authority and generally keeping the morale and social tone in well-worked tension. The chief encourages building traditionally designed houses and is at great pains to show his people how they can be prosperous through agriculture, but even so, how long are his people going to continue a communitarian way of life in which he and the other major chiefs get most of the money and dole it out as they think best for the *aiga?* There are already signs aplenty in his village of people living in the privacy of the *palagi*-style house with their own individual sources of income.

We visited Aoloau on Easter Sunday. After services in the church house, the village elders had a feast in the main room. We sat on traditional mats but the mats were on a linoleum floor. The food was the same mixture of the new and the old. Roast pork, taro, red snapper cooked in coconut cream, but also chicken and ice cream and commercially baked cookies. The women and the young people served but did not eat with us, yet the old men of the village council, the power establishment, chiefs, members of the *fono* and ministers, told us it was heavy going against the TV.

It's not just that the box introduces individualist values but it breaks up the schedule of family and community life. Supper and the early evenings are used for togetherness but also for discussing problems and planning tomorrow's work, which isn't easy to do if the workers are looking at the tube while it blats out "Columbo" and "McMillan and Wife." The trail down that mountain leads to dropping frozen waffles into the toasters, Franco-American SpaghettiOs, and the American family eating habits, with every member of the family dining at a different hour, with its own age group, popping precooked inorganic substances into an infrared oven for warming-up. Sorry about your civilization fellas, but our gadgets are better than your gadgets.

Fui'a has lived in Washington. He knows what America is about and in the back of his mind he must be thinking the jig is up. "I'm against the gambling casino, I'm against the oil refinery. It would take five hundred acres of level land which we need for farming and houses. Someday we may have to have it but one accident and it's finished, *uma*, finished, *uma*, that's our word for it."

I hate to tell you, chief, but it's *uma* for you. They're playing "Kung Fu vs. The Godfather" (rated PG) at a local movie house. It can't be *uma* fast enough for Nita Tolmi. She's the assistant director of Gas's Material Management Office, the outfit that is most frequently blamed for ordering ten thousand bottles of whiskey in special American Samoa commemorative decanters for the government-run liquor store monopoly. Samoans, who if the figures are right (a per capita booze consumption of fifty-three gallons), will drink anything, have refused to help Gas get rid of the decanters. They're holding out for Chivas Regal which is in short supply at the monopoly store.

Nita is definitely part of the Rotarian conspiracy with Herb and Sherry. She thinks Sadie Thompson was a bisexual and she says, "I'm sick and tired of that goddamn *fono* saying *palagi* go home but leave your wallet. We've had a silver spoon in our mouths for seventy-five years. What we need is to get off the take and get on to a program." Nita ordered another drink and continued. "Now our office has just done a study of all the studies that have been done of Samoa. It goes on and on."

"It sure does," Garrybaldi mumbled.

"For real freedom, you have to belong to the world. We have to realize we can't go back to planting taro and catching fish."

"I'm hungry," said Garrybaldi.

"Okay," Nita responded, "stick out your tongue and I'll tell you how much I'll charge you."

"That wasn't exactly what I had in mind," Michael J. Doonesbury's father said, getting up, knowing yet one more meal in the Rain Maker dining room was being cooked for him. It would be one of the last. Our time was up. We were past due. The Virgin Flooze had taken Christian shopping— she was spending a lot of time buying Polynesian print material, very authentic stuff flown in from the textile mills of North Carolina—and in the store she'd heard Christian say to himself, "Those big brown people want to hit me."

Liz and the Flooze had gone to call on Mrs. Foots, and while the effect had been healthy it hadn't lasted. The Flooze, who'd spent her adolescence observing the more dangerous forms of violent degeneracy in Tapanga Canyon, was unable to see in Mrs. Foots what Liz remembered from Louisiana days. White woman, Southern, Mrs. Foots could not only endure and maintain, but summerize Western civilization in her conduct of the kitchen. "The gas for the stove was off— this island!—but that woman crawled around and found a can of sterno to cook with. She cannot unmake history but she can get up and make cookies for a movie star toddling by in the morning. She can't get these people out of their palm trees and teach them to walk on two feet but she can take care of her family. She cannot undo history, she cannot rewrite the Constitution, but she can run a home and she does. That woman walked eight weeks every two years when her husband was running for Congress, and do you know what she told me? She told me she'd given away forty thousand candy bars (the Baby Ruths which were Foots's trademark), but she said 'I never gave one away unless they'd shake my hand because I believe in the human touch.' The human touch, crawl on the floor to find the sterno. She did it again this last election. Walked and walked and gave away the candy bars. 'But it was just useless this time,' she said. Useless. What are we doing on this island?"

In addition to being a Hollywood type and famous, Liz is a great actress. They say Sarah Bernhardt could make you weep reciting the multiplication tables, but I never believed it until I heard Liz describing having cookies with Mrs. Foots at eleven o'clock in the morning in the kitchen. It's true, great acting has nothing to do with the words. Liz can take any emotion, ball it up inside her into the shape of a projectile and propel it into you. It had happened to me once before with her. That time I thought it was the grass or something. When she finished I was weeping, I was taking the most ordinary events of my life—loading the dishwasher, listening to a jerk politician—and I w-a-s s-o s-a-d.

Now I was s-o s-a-d again. I don't know why. She had me feel the tragedy of the South and that linked up with our coming here, our mission. We had come wanting to give of ourselves and we had been stripped by the bellhops. We had come offering that which we had, and we had been robbed by room service, we had arrived committed, dedicated, and been mugged by an enormous greenish-yellow palm-like piece of vegetation on whose leaves Garrybaldi would write notes, tear them off, and slip them under the Flooze's door, but the goddamn thing would grow a new and bigger leaf within an hour.

We had been repudiated. "I am a tart, I am a hussy, I am a slat-TERN," Liz wailed and I wailed with her. We were on the balcony once more. The Flooze was looking off through the mist and the giant splotches of rain that were coming down at odd angles as though God were a little boy who'd filled his mouth up at a water bubbler and was blowing out at us. Like the little heads of the men at the four corners of old maps spitting foul weather across the Mercator projection.

"Well, I keep coming back to it," Garrybaldi told us, "I didn't get a suntan, I didn't send my postcards, my friends will think I've been in Toledo, Ohio. How can you come back from nine days in the tropics, south of the equator too, and look like I do? I can tell my friends I lost my address book, but I don't think that'll work with my mother."

Davidson was expatiating on the coconut terror. "People are killed by falling coconuts all the time here. A ripe coconut is several times harder than the human skull, although perhaps not a Samoan skull. Legend has it that a coconut fell on the

head of a High Talking Chief and split open which was how coconut milk was discovered. The reason the coconut is so terrible is that it is the largest single cell known to botany or biology."

"I don't want to be in jungle movies," Liz said, pleading with the American Eagle. "I'm a backlot ac-TRESS. I cannot swing from trees. I don't believe in it. We're patriots! Oh, God, just a few weeks ago, I was a star."

"Different set of constellations here. Have you seen the Southern cross?" Davidson wanted to know.

"I am not a telescope. I can't see through clouds. Oh, McCarthy, McCarthy, am I going to die here?" Liz asked, throwing her arms out and falling on McCarthy.

Instead of dying we made our way in the rain through the jumble of houses and shacks of Fagatogo to have dinner at Herb and Sia's motel, where Rosey was waiting on tables and the nieces were back in their grass skirts. The Flooze, at long last with an opportunity to strut her stuff, jumped on the piano and sang, which revived our spirits somewhat, but not for long. The mildew had reached our brains. We made our way back to the Americana like bugs that had been sprayed by DDT, where we packed as though we'd been ordered to evacuate, flung ourselves into taxicabs, and fled to the airport where Liz and I fought with porters, the ticket agents, the immigration officials, the gate agents, and the baggage handlers. The Flooze was collapsed on the bench, half draped over Davidson, who was spotless and pressed in his white suit, even though he had that book out and was looking at the triangulated and mummified genitalia of deceased Egyptian royalty. He kept saying that when he got back to Washington he was going to form a committee, not to liberate Samoa, but to kick it out of the American commonwealth. Garrybaldi tried to keep our morale up and told us not to be candy asses, but he was coming down with hot and cold running trots and was worrying we'd have to watch the same Mel Brooks movie Pan Am had shown on the way out. We told him that Red Cross emergency rescue flights didn't show movies.

When it came time to board, they wouldn't let McCarthy

carry his guitar with him. Liz said that if they didn't change their minds she'd run 'em all back up into the trees and hang them by their necks with their own tails and don't tell me I'm a racist, I got my ticket punched at Selma when you people were still chasing each other around trying to eat your mother's big toes.

None of us spoke until we landed in Hawaii. At the customs inspection they asked us if we had anything to declare and I remember telling the agent, "There really isn't much you can say about an island of bisexual, polygamous cannibals." "No, sir, I mean do you have anything to declare, did you bring anything with you from American Samoa?" "Good god, I hope not . . . Although I do have a sore throat and this strange itch . . . "